World Economics Association

Book Series

Volume

D1441002

40 Critical Pointers for
Students of Economics

Titles produced by the World Economics Association & College Publications

Volume 2
Finance as Warfare
Michael Hudson

Volume 3
Developing an economics for the post-crisis world
Steve Keen

Volume 4
On the use and misuse of theories and models in mainstream economics
Lars Pålsson Syll

Volume 5
Green Capitalism. The God that Failed
Richard Smith

Volume 6
40 Critical Pointers for Students of Economics
Stuart Birks

The **World Economics Association (WEA)** was launched on May 16, 2011. Already over 13,000 economists and related scholars have joined. This phenomenal success has come about because the WEA fills a huge gap in the international community of economists – the absence of a professional organization which is truly international and pluralist.

The World Economics Association seeks to increase the relevance, breadth and depth of economic thought. Its key qualities are worldwide membership and governance, and inclusiveness with respect to: (a) the variety of theoretical perspectives; (b) the range of human activities and issues which fall within the broad domain of economics; and (c) the study of the world's diverse economies.

The Association's activities centre on the development, promotion and diffusion of economic research and knowledge and on illuminating their social character.

The WEA publishes 20+ books a year, three open-access journals (*Economic Thought*, *World Economic Review* and *Real-World Economics Review*), a bi-monthly newsletter, blogs, holds global online conferences, runs a textbook commentaries project and an eBook library.

www.worldeconomicassociation.org

40 Critical Pointers for Students of Economics

Stuart Birks

© Stuart Birks, WEA and College Publications 2016.

All rights reserved.

ISBN 978-1-84890-217-6 print
ISBN 978-1-911156-05-5 eBook-PDF

Published by College Publications on behalf of the World Economics Association

http://www.worldeconomicsassociation.org
http://www.collegepublications.co.uk

Printed by Lightning Source, Milton Keynes, UK

40 critical pointers for students of economics

Contents

POLICY

POLICY APPLICATIONS

Introduction

Most of the economics texts and courses taught around the world focus on what is sometimes termed mainstream economics. These courses train students to view the world according to a particular, primarily neoclassical framing. It is important to know this approach because it has come to be seen as a basis for understanding the real world. It shapes the way many people now think. Kuhn (1970, p. 5) described "normal science" research, or the research done by the majority of people in a discipline or profession, as "a strenuous and devoted attempt to force nature into the conceptual boxes supplied by a professional education". Training conditions people to see things in a particular way, selecting the components to be emphasised and those to be excluded, and describing the relationships between the chosen elements.

Economics texts often claim that their content originates in the works of Adam Smith, author of the *Wealth of Nations* and the "father of economics", although he might be shocked by current representations of his ideas. The so called "invisible hand" has been repeatedly overemphasised and misrepresented, and the current representation of markets emphasises equilibrium, a word that Smith never used in the *Wealth of Nations*.

Not only does mainstream economics dominate, but courses in recent decades have increasingly focused on selected models and quantitative research methods, primarily econometrics. Some would counter this point by referring to game theory, experimental economics and behavioural economics, but these could be seen as developments within rather than a broadening of the framework.

Many of the reservations and qualifications that used to be presented in descriptions of theory have now been dropped, especially as the length and content of courses have been reduced. Consequently there has been a narrowing down of the discipline. Little is said of real world aspects except to the extent that models may give some explanation that is consistent with what is observed. Of course, the models also give a framing of the issues such that the explanations are largely predetermined by the selection of the models.

It is important to know the limitations of this approach. However, for many students these limitations are given scant attention. This book introduces you to 40 critical pointers for those who wish to see the theory in a broader, more realistic context. The material draws on supplementary course material that I have developed and used over the past 30 years or so. It is suitable for introductory and intermediate courses and can be included selectively by students for additional reading or in lectures or tutorials as discussion points. Related resources, including some of these pointers, can be found online as individual pages in the World Economics Association's: **Textbook Commentaries Project** at: www.worldeconomicsassociation.org.

The broader underlying philosophy has been pulled together in a publication primarily suited to graduate students, academics and researchers, *Rethinking economics: from analogies to the real world* (Birks, 2015).

Core economics

1. A market-focused world

Mainstream economics starts with a default position of a theoretical world that is reliant on markets for the allocation of resources. These markets involve the coming together of producers (supply) and consumers (demand) in a static representation where all demand over a period of time and all supply over that period of time is considered to occur simultaneously (more precisely, there is no time dimension in the representation so time differences are ignored and timing is assumed to be irrelevant). It is then argued that an "optimal" structure is one of universal perfect competition. On this basis, it is further claimed that there is "market failure" when this optimum is not achieved, and this may justify government intervention.

The theoretical world is comprised of individual consumers who aim to maximise their utility and individual firms which aim to maximise their profits. Imagine this world. Utility is maximised solely through the consumption of goods and services. Individual firms are single-mindedly profit maximising. We should recognise that the same self-interested individuals who are maximising their own utility are also grouping together in firms so as to cooperate optimally in the process of profit maximising. Moreover, while competition is ruthless between firms, cooperation is absolute within firms, and everyone is law abiding and respects each other's property rights, which are well-defined.

Traditionally it would have been said of such an approach that it considers some aspects of society only. It is therefore only a partial analysis, with other things "taken as given", fixed, determined outside the model. The model is therefore only assisting in understanding a component of the real world, and its limitations should be recognised. More recently some textbooks present this theory as if it is sufficient on its own as a description of the real world.

This is surprising, given the many ways in which it differs from reality. Many aspects are assumed away. Hence it is assumed that we can use this body of theory to analyse a real world which includes a large public sector as well as legal, political, religious, military, educational, cultural and other institutions, all of which are changing over time. Other ways of observing society may provide alternative insights and highlight other important issues. These alternative framings could include numerous actual, or perceived/socially constructed divisions and hierarchies, including class, ethnicity, age, gender, and religion. Groups, communities and families may be important influences on behaviour. Moreover, there are conflicts within and between countries, resulting in political, economic, legal and military action. The economy is not everything and it does not exist in a vacuum.

2. Static analysis

Even if not explicitly stated, mainstream economics relies heavily on static analysis. Economic models of supply and demand, consumer utility maximisation, firm production and cost decisions and profit maximisation, macroeconomic models of aggregate demand and aggregate supply, equilibrium and multipliers and many more are examples of static analysis. These have no time dimension. They could be considered to represent activity over some period of time, where totals are given but the actual timing is ignored. As with any framing, this shapes what we see and what is overlooked.

To illustrate, imagine a market for a good, with all the people who might supply the good and all the people who might want to buy the good present in a room. In static analysis, it is as if the door is then locked. Nobody is able to enter or leave until agreement is reached whereby the amount to be supplied equals the amount people wish to buy. Assume, in addition, that this equals exactly the quantity which has been produced (although this quantity was indeterminate beforehand). No trades occur until agreement is reached. All trades then take place at the agreed price and the people can leave the room.

Clearly this is does not describe real world markets. In practice it is as if people can enter and leave at any time. They can only trade when they are in the room, but trades can and do occur without overall agreement on price being reached. The concept of an equilibrium price is meaningless in this environment. At any point, trades may occur. These are at the prevailing price or a price agreed between a specific buyer and seller, even though this may differ from prices offered elsewhere at the same time. Some may decide not to buy or sell at the prevailing price even though they might have been prepared to trade at some fictitious equilibrium price. They may leave the market and not return. Over time, the participants in the market are changing and it is by no means certain that the same price would equate demand and supply for all groups of participants.

Adam Smith did not use the term "equilibrium price", or even the word "equilibrium", in the *Wealth of Nations* (Smith, 2007 [1776]). Instead, in Book 1, Chapter 7 he talked of a "natural price", describing it as, "as it were, the central price to which the prices of all commodities are continually gravitating". The specific circumstances faced by traders at any one time will influence current and may shape subsequent behaviour, but trades are unlikely to all occur at some single price that equates demand and supply over the whole term of the market.

The process of price determination or price adjustment is not specified in the static analysis of a market, but in the real world it may be very important. Institutional factors can be crucial for determining behaviour. To give one extreme situation, many products are sold at a fixed, centrally determined price, as when companies advertise through the mass media specifying a price. Such prices may be seldom adjusted, with little or no regard for locational differences. At the other extreme, in some cultures and places of sale bargaining is expected. In such a situation the price at which an item is sold is specific to the individual transaction. Auctions, including online auctions, further complicate matters. Even with outlets such as supermarkets which sell at a set price, prices may vary by the day or week and they may differ over stores or chains at any one time. It is hard to see how this fits a static representation of a market.

Similar reasoning applies in other situations where static analysis is commonly applied. We live in a dynamic, ever changing environment. The focus in this section has been on supply and demand, but equivalent considerations would apply elsewhere, including production decisions by a firm or macroeconomic analysis of, for example, fiscal or monetary policy [see also No.4].

3. Comparative static analysis

Where one static situation is given, this is called **static analysis**. Where two static situations are compared, it is an example of **comparative static analysis**. For example, there could be a comparison of a market with and without a per unit tax on units supplied, or of the market for cars before and after a rise in the price of petrol.

Static and comparative static analysis both focus on equilibria and optima. Note that, as comparative static analysis simply compares two static situations. It says nothing about which, if either, is the current real world position, or if there are any issues of adjustment from one to the other static position. Consequently, if the analysis is used to consider movement to one of two or more alternatives, it only compares the nature of the theoretical outcomes, with no regard for the feasibility or costs of moving to these outcomes. Similarly, if one situation is a starting point and another is an end point, the issue of behaviour when moving between these positions, essentially the process of adjustment, is not included in the theory. In reality adjustment issues can be very important. If adjustment to equilibrium is slow, then the real world experience is likely to be one of disequilibrium. This also means that policy changes which alter equilibria will result in adjustment patterns which take time and could have significant implications. Consequently, it may not be enough to think only of behaviour when everyone has fully adjusted to the change. The timing, path and costs of adjustment, including the possibly uneven distribution of costs, are important.

Imagine if we are at one equilibrium position and consider an alternative equilibrium to be preferred. It is not enough simply to set up the conditions for the second and then expect the adjustment to occur. We have to actually move from one to the other. This can take time and involve costs. The term "transition economies" refers to the economies of the former Soviet Union, which went through a transition to rely more on markets for resource allocation decisions. It has not been a smooth and simple adjustment. For a very readable description of the problems they faced in this process of change, see Hare (2012).

Many textbooks argue that free trade is desirable because it allows for optimal specialisation and maximum gains from trade. Major shifts in production from some countries to others also change employment patterns and reduce returns to past investment in physical and human capital in the source countries. These costs would not be there if the later production patterns had existed from the beginning, and they can be significant for those who are directly affected. This is not to say that the changes should not occur, but simply that comparative static analysis fails to consider these aspects.

We should also be open to the possibility that it may not be possible to reach one static position from another. Imagine a starting point sitting in a plane and an alternative point on the ground immediately below the plane. The process of adjustment might be an important consideration if the only way to achieve the latter is to jump out of the plane without a parachute.

Moreover, there can also be efficiency, equity and incentive effects arising from the change. For example, a change in some subsidies or taxes can alter expectations about future income/benefit streams to land or capital assets. One way to calculate the value of assets is to compute the present value of their future net benefits. The expected effect of taxes or subsidies on income/benefit streams can be capitalised as reductions (in the case of taxes) or increases (in the case of subsidies) in capital values. If calculated correctly, all the losses or gains impact on the owner at the time of the change in the form of a capital loss or capital gain.

Briefly, then, static and hence comparative static analysis cannot say much about processes of change. This is a limitation of the approach. Comparative static analysis takes a "blank sheet of paper" approach to each equilibrium or optimum, where all adjustments are assumed to have taken place and with no regard for any costs of adjustment. It considers the before and after situations without regard for **path dependence**. An alternative perspective is to take a historical view in which the course of events through time is central, as with **historical institutionalism** (Steinmo, 2008) for example.

4. Supply and demand

There are similarities between the description of market demand curves and market supply curves. For both, there are several determinants, one of them, price, getting special emphasis in graphical depictions of markets. Consequently this determinant generates movements along the curve. The other determinants cause shifts in demand/supply. The pattern of analysis involves holding all but one determinant constant and seeing what happens as that variable (in this case price) changes. This is a way to systematically consider the impact of each variable. If two or more determinants change at the same time, it is not possible to separate out their effects. We know that, in the real world, many things change simultaneously. There is an assumption that we can consider individual effects in isolation, and we can then combine them to consider more complex situations.

In complex systems many variables may affect each other, so this form of analysis may not be realistic. Consequently there are unstated assumptions implicit in its use. Consider, for example, tastes and income as determinants of demand. If tastes change with income, should they be considered in isolation? Can we consider the additional production of bread from an extra baker if no more flour is used?

There is a focus on price in the diagrams, and this may shape our perceptions, but the other determinants are also important. In the real world competition is not just price competition between producers of identical items. There is product differentiation, branding, competition on service, and competition in the development of new products (consider mobile phones or tablets, for example).

There is a difference between the simplified theoretical representation of a market and the real world environments in which goods and services are traded. Consider what we might actually observe in a market – we do not see complete demand and supply curves. Instead, we might observe certain points indicating prices and perhaps quantities traded over a period of time (although firms may be unwilling to disclose this information). Individual suppliers might know their own sales, but not those of their competitors.

Even if we know price and sales in a market, this may not give us equilibrium points. One suggestion based on the static model of a market is that we would just see the "short" side of the market (the supply curve for prices up to the equilibrium price and the demand curve for prices higher than equilibrium).

We may not be observing any excess demand or excess supply, assuming that these theoretical constructs can be realised. If you wish to buy something but do not see it in the shops, do you express your demand to the suppliers, wait until it is available, or decide to do/buy something else? Unemployment is sometimes referred to as excess supply of labour. If you cannot get a job of a particular type, do you continue applying for jobs, do nothing and wait for the job market to improve, take some other type of job that comes available, or decide to do something else such as leave the labour market and undertake further study, or become a homemaker? There are many ways that people can respond. Perhaps the textbooks place too much emphasis on price and too little on other determinants and options.

There is more to be considered when thinking of real world markets, such as the information available and how it is conveyed, the ways in which adjustments can occur, the importance of distance and location in setting the geographical boundaries of markets, etc. Also bear in mind the importance of property rights, trust, contracts, etc., in other words, institutional aspects.

For more discussion of supply and demand, you could look at Birks (2014).

5. Marginalism

Much of standard optimisation found in neoclassical economics relies on calculus to determine the optimal conditions. It is apparent where ever you see a differential, or terms that include the word "marginal" such as marginal cost, marginal revenue, marginal utility, marginal productivity, marginal revenue product, or marginal rate of substitution.

Calculus is only really applicable where small (marginal) changes can occur. Conceptually, the general rule is then that, if a small change is beneficial, make that change then consider another small change. Continue until no further gain is observed, at which point you have reached an optimum (a maximum or a minimum depending on your objective).

Strictly speaking, all we can then say is that we have met the first order condition for a local optimum. Second order conditions are necessary to determine whether it is a maximum, a minimum or a saddle point (in which case it is neither a maximum nor a minimum). Consider a function as illustrated in Figure 1.

Figure 1

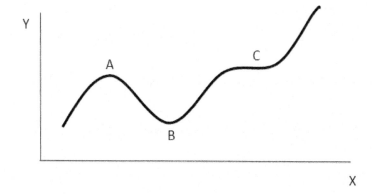

Point A gives a maximum, point B a minimum and point C a saddle point.

There may be several optima, in which case the marginal rule will take you to a local one, but this may not be the global (overall) optimum (observe that point A does not give the highest possible value of Y, higher points can be achieved for values of X to the right of point C). This could be a problem, but there is another more serious problem.

It may be that, for a particular application, small adjustments are not possible. The representation is then flawed. Consider a consumer deciding how many cars to buy. The available options are none, one, perhaps two and, less likely, three. Many items are like this. For them, marginal analysis gives a poor representation of the optimisation problem.

We can see this in the case of production, where marginal rules are applied in the standard diagram in capital-labour space using isoquants and an iso-cost line. Nicely curved isoquants assume that it is possible to continuously substitute one factor for another while maintaining the same output level.

Consider a different situation where there are a limited number of production options, each with a fixed capital-labour ratio. For each form of transport there is a fixed vehicle-driver requirement. It is not possible to substitute buses for drivers, or vice versa. Figure 2 illustrates this situation for buses, with increasing numbers of passengers as we move further from the origin along the ray labelled "bus", and similarly for minibuses and taxis.

Figure 2

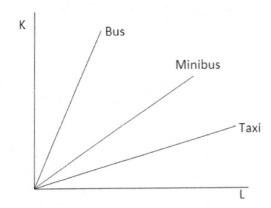

To be more accurate, it is only possible to have whole vehicles, so the rays should really be dotted lines with vehicles sometimes having empty seats (unless our measure is something like passenger-kilometres per hour), but we will overlook that. If we assume that doubling the number of vehicles and drivers would double the output, then we would observe constant returns to scale along the rays. It is possible to operate at points between these rays by using 2 buses and 3 minibuses, for example. This means that we can construct iosquants. With constant returns to scale for each mode of transport, isoquants would have linear sections between the rays. For example, if a bus can carry 50 passengers and a minibus can carry 10, then we could carry 100 passengers on 2 buses, or on 10 minibuses, or on a combination of 1 bus and 5 minibuses. One such isoquant is shown in Figure 3.

Figure 3

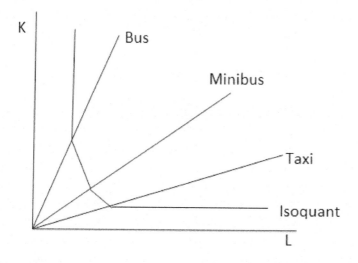

Cost minimisation or output maximisation with this structure would be represented mathematically as a linear programming problem, not one using calculus. The solution has different characteristics. There is not gradual adjustment to find a point of tangency between an isoquant and an isocost line. The solution is still at a point where the two lines just touch, but this would generally be where an isoquant changes slope, in which case the slope of the isocost line could lie anywhere between the slopes of the two sections of the isoquant. If the isocost line has the same slope as a section of the isoquant, then any point on the section will give the same outcome and there are multiple solutions. An added difference between resource allocation problems suited to calculus and those suited to linear programming is that with calculus we expect all resources to be used. With linear programming some resources may be left unused, we cannot apply them in place of something else. You may have buses available, but no drivers, or drivers available but no taxis, for example.

There is a key point to take from this. Far from being a broad and generally applicable representation of production options, standard analysis using isoquants and marginality may be a special case describing the extreme situation where there is an infinite number of viable alternative technologies from which to choose. In reality there are likely to be a limited number of such technologies and, perhaps, of scales of production. Similar points could be made for consumption activities, noting that activities can include combinations of goods and services, perhaps in fixed proportions.

6. Diminishing marginal utility, relievers and pleasers

Textbooks generally emphasise the existence and importance of diminishing marginal utility. It is an important mathematical requirement for the standard conclusions on the behaviour of utility maximising individuals. An alternative possibility is described by Charles Karelis (2007), illustrated through his description of the effects of bee stings.

Consider being stung several times. The first sting may be very painful, but after that, a second, third or seventh, while still adding to the pain and discomfort, is of somewhat less importance: "The sting on the hand would be like a shout that is striking in a quiet street but hardly noticed in a riot" (Karelis, 2007, p.68). Now consider this in reverse. Imagine that there is a salve that, when applied to a sting, can completely relieve it. When applied to the seventh sting, leaving six, there is some slight reduction in discomfort, like quieting a shout in a riot. In contrast, the effect of the salve on the last sting is like quieting a shout in a quiet street. "Doubtless you would pay much more for a single dab in that situation." As Karelis describes it, "if the marginal misery produced by stings is diminishing, then the marginal relief produced by dabs of salve must be increasing."

This is different from the standard type of good that you will come across in economics textbooks. Karelis defines two types of good. The standard ones that display diminishing marginal utility he calls "pleasers". Another type of good, such as the salve, Karelis calls "relievers". The marginal benefit of these increases (until there is no more relief to be obtained).

Karelis takes his analysis a step further by describing goods which can be both relievers and pleasers. He calls these "reliever/pleasers". Instead of simply considering utility from consumption, imagine the following three possible levels of consumption of "basic" goods (such as food, clothing, or shelter). For the first level, they could be consumed in insufficient quantities, where consumption gives relief from hunger or cold, say. At the second level, consumption is sufficient, giving neither discomfort nor pleasure, and at the third level pleasure can be obtained by consuming more, or better quality.

It is through consideration of this category of reliever/pleasers that Karelis suggests that policies intended to encourage people out of poverty may be less effective than commonly assumed. He contends that someone on very low income may not respond strongly to incentives to earn. This is because initial earnings simply provide for reliever consumption. Someone on very low income may require a big increase in income to be relieved of discomfort, so a small incentive may give little relief. There would be so much discomfort remaining that the benefit might not seem worth the effort.

There is a parallel to this (but in a different dimension) with the concept of the **"poverty trap"**. People on low income may receive income-related benefits such as an accommodation supplement. As their income rises, not only do they pay tax on the extra income, but also their benefits reduce. The net income gain may be very small. (If you consider the reduction in benefits as a form of tax, you will understand why we sometimes refer to the overall effect on an extra dollar's income as an "effective marginal tax rate".) In some extreme cases an extra dollar of income can result in tax payments and reduced benefits that exceed a dollar, so that disposable income actually falls!

Both of these concepts (reliever/pleasers and the poverty trap) suggest that people in poverty may need to see the possibility of a major change in circumstances if they are to have an incentive to improve their position.

7. Gains from trade

You will generally see the potential benefits of trade described in terms of comparative advantage and a suitable price ratio for mutually beneficial exchange. This principle can be applied to countries, as is commonly discussed, but it applies equally to any form of specialisation and exchange, including that between regions, towns, or individuals and for decisions on resource use, such as the use of land.

Introductory economics texts frequently make the claim that international trade can make everyone better off. This is based on the ability of trade to allow positions to be achieved that are outside a country's production possibility frontier. Using comparative static analysis, we can see that a country fully adjusted to a situation with international trade generally[1] has more options than one without international trade. If wellbeing is measured purely in relation to availability of goods and services, where greater availability increase wellbeing, then the claim that trade is beneficial is supported. We should note that this is using comparative statics to compare trade to no trade. In itself, the claim may be plausible, but it is important to see what is omitted by reliance on this reasoning alone.

Even under static analysis, when comparing the two options nothing is said about related differences in:

   i.   types of work involved;
   ii.   environmental impacts of the patterns of production;

---

[1] Might there be gains from trade if all countries are identical? Could the answer depend on the presence of economies of scale?

iii.   economic, political or strategic vulnerability; or

iv.   the distribution of income and wealth within the countries.

On types of work, note the following quote from Adam Smith's *Wealth of Nations*, describing the effects of specialisation, the division of labour and repeated performance of routine operations:

> "The man whose whole life is spent in performing a few simple operations, of which the effects are perhaps always the same, or very nearly the same, has no occasion to exert his understanding or to exercise his invention in finding out expedients for removing difficulties which never occur... His dexterity at his own particular trade seems... to be acquired at the expense of his intellectual, social, and martial virtues" (Smith, 2007 [1776], Book V Chapter 1).

Also a policy decision to move from no trade to trade involves starting at the no trade situation, with its historic structure of capital stock, skills and so on, and finding an adjustment path as the economy adapts to the presence of trade. These changes have time and monetary costs, as well as redistributive effects. There are alternative paths that could be followed, influenced in part by policy decisions. Some buildings, plant and machinery and some skills will be in less demand than before, possibly then being unemployed (note the difference between the **physical and economic life** [No. 36] of an asset).

In reality the issue is not generally one of international trade or no international trade, but rather one of the form and extent of any barriers to trade such as tariffs or quotas. While standard economic theory may be helpful for analysing such options, it should be noted that the **Theory of Second Best** [No. 16] could be important.

The possibility of distributional implications is illustrated by the so-called "**Dutch disease**". Named after the experience of Holland, rapid growth in one sector (as from the discovery and exploitation of oil or gas reserves) can push up the exchange rate, thereby harming other sectors.

Rostow indicated some of the factors to be considered for an economy in the process of moving from a fairly traditional (non-industrialised) state, attempting to "take off" to become a modern economy. He identified the need for, "psychological, social, technological, and institutional changes" (Rostow, 1971, p. 100). This is why he described the adjustment as one of "take off" into self-sustained growth. Major changes would be needed in these areas for the economy to reach and stay in the more prosperous state, so marginal adjustments alone would fail to do this. Note also the discussion of relievers and pleasers and the poverty trap [in No.6].

Texts commonly focus on comparative advantage, which is presented with given (fixed) production possibilities. This assumption may not apply in the real world. In fact, patterns of comparative advantage are changing all the time. It may be possible to have policies which generate favourable changes for a country. This has been recognised for a long time, although generally not in introductory economics texts. Theories of comparative advantage tend to consider prevailing endowments. Another perspective is described by Ojimi, who was at the Japanese Ministry of International Trade and Industry (MITI) (Eatwell, 1987). After the Second World War Japan recognised that its future according to comparative advantage would result in low incomes and slow growth. Recognising an alternative option if it could become competitive in high value added, high growth industries, it used a combination of policies to eventually achieve highly competitive car and electronics production. In other words, comparative advantage can be endogenous.

> "From a short-run, static viewpoint, encouragement of such industries would seem to be in conflict with economic rationalism. But from a long-range viewpoint, these are precisely in industries where income elasticity of demand is high, technological progress is rapid, and labour productivity rises fast ..." (Ojimi, 1970).

Michael Porter gained publicity for promoting the concept of **competitive advantage** (Porter, 2004). This term refers to the possibility that comparative advantage is not predetermined, but can be changed, as occurred in Japan. Porter placed particular emphasis on the role of competition in this process, hence his name for the concept. Focus on competition through investment, technological change and innovation is not new. A similar point was made by Schumpeter (1976, pp. 81-86) in his concept of **creative destruction**. These concepts are based on a more dynamic representation of the issues that is seen in the use of static analysis to describe comparative advantage.

Also, in a perhaps telling point given recent experience in many countries, Linder (Linder, 1977, p. 250) describes "...the theory of comparative advantages, which decrees that in the long run it is better for a nation to sacrifice an entire industry in order to put its scarce resources to more efficient use."

8. Producer and consumer surplus and gains from economic activity

Here is a standard diagram used to illustrate producer surplus (PS) and consumer surplus (CS).

Figure 4

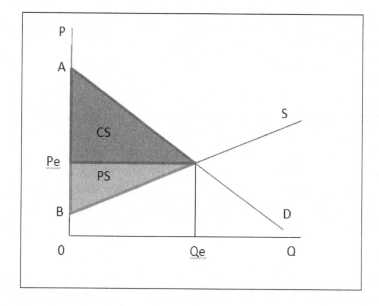

We should remember that demand and supply curves are unlikely to be straight lines, so this is a highly stylised representation even if we accept a static depiction of a market.

1. Consider the area under the demand curve from the vertical axis to the equilibrium quantity. This consists of the blue triangle plus a rectangle with height equal to the equilibrium price, Pe, and width equal to the equilibrium quantity, Qe. The area of the rectangle, being Pe x Qe, is equal to the total amount paid by consumers for those goods or services. If we were to start selling on the market by offering one unit, someone would be prepared to pay a price 0A for that single unit. If we then offered another unit, it could be sold for a price slightly lower, and so on, unit by unit until we get to the equilibrium quantity, with the last unit being sold at the equilibrium price. In other words, consumers would be prepared to pay the amount that they do pay, Pe x Qe, plus the area of the blue triangle, labelled "consumer surplus", the extra benefit that consumers obtain over and above what they have to pay. Similarly for suppliers, they may be induced to supply a first unit at a price 0B, and so on using the area under the supply curve up to the equilibrium point. They actually receive the whole rectangle, so they are receiving a producer surplus, a sum over and above that required for them to supply the equilibrium quantity. For various reasons **these are just approximations**[2], but they indicate that the net benefits from the activity of producing and consuming the good or service should not be measured as the amount spent, Pe x Qe, but by measuring benefits minus costs. This is approximately the area in the diagram represented by the two triangles for consumer and producer surplus. We do not observe these in reality and might not expect to be able to calculate them. However, the concepts should indicate that commonly used measures of output, income, consumption, etc., are not good measures of net benefit to society. They are based on market prices which, at best, reflect circumstances at the margin.

---

[2] Note that if consumers paid the higher prices for the initial units they would have less income to buy additional units. Consequently there is the concept of a "compensated demand curve".

From the above reasoning it can be concluded that price times quantity is a poor measure of the net benefit to society of the operation of a competitive market even in the absence of externalities. Consequently macroeconomic aggregates based on such a measure for all markets, irrespective of whether they are competitive, are also poor measures of the value of economic activity. PxQ does not reflect net benefit, nor does it measure either costs or benefits. Other than it being relatively convenient to calculate, it is hard to know what value it really has for analysis. Nevertheless it assumes great importance in research, the news media and political debate.

You may be wondering who gets the producer surplus in perfectly competitive markets, where only normal profits are obtained. Imagine an industry facing an increase in demand. It is already employing workers, but may have to pay more to increase its labour force. This would result in existing workers also getting a rise in pay. In this example, some of the surplus would go to workers in wages, rather than to the firm in profits. Similar changes can occur in returns to capital or in land prices (think of the rise in the price of central city land as a city expands). This phenomenon is sometimes referred to as **economic rent**.

9. The circular flow and the quantity theory of money

The Quantity Theory of Money is based on the relationship

M x V = P x Q

where M, V, P and Q represent, respectively, **M**oney supply, the **V**elocity of circulation, the **P**rice level, and real GDP (**Q**, or, in some versions, **Y)**).

An earlier version dating back several centuries, but more recently linked to Fisher, is **M x V = P x T**, where T represents transactions and the other variables have the same meaning as above.[3] In this form it states that the

---

[3] These "Quantity equations" are discussed in section 2.2 of Friedman and Schwartz Friedman, M. & Schwartz, A. J. 1982. *Monetary trends in the United States and the United Kingdom, their relation to income, prices, and interest rates, 1867-1975.*

amount of money paid for goods and services is equal to the monetary value of all goods and services given in transactions. Hence, it is an identity, it always true. The substitution of Q for T requires a redefinition of V. It can no longer be the number of times a unit of currency is used in transactions in a period. It is sometimes explained in terms of the Circular Flow of Income, where $P \times Q$ = nominal GDP.

In the circular flow diagram all output of final goods and services is purchased, with income equalling expenditure. The flow of final goods and services in one direction is matched by a flow of money in the other. This is represented by $M \times V = P \times Q$. It by no means represents all the transactions, however. There is also a flow of factor services (labour, etc.) from households to firms, and factor payments (wages, etc.) in the reverse direction. As income equals expenditure, this also totals $P \times Q$ (ignoring minor timing differences for the two flows of payments). Consequently, transactions in relation to production and distribution of final goods and services alone would equal $2 \times P \times Q$.

In addition, production can involve many **intermediate transactions** such as the purchase and sale of components at various stages in the production process. These arise because outputs are not always sold as final demand. Some outputs become inputs elsewhere. The final price reflects the sum of value added at various stages in the production process, whereas the related transactions include the full value of earlier inputs. The total value of transactions in the production of a good can be much greater than the final price.

Transactions also occur with the sale of second-hand goods, existing houses, etc. These transactions bear little or no relationship to currently produced final goods and services (only a small part of the sale price of real estate is for the current services of estate agents, for example). We could also factor in transfer payments, where money flows in one direction without a reciprocal flow of goods or services in the other.

Chicago, University of Chicago Press. Note especially pp.23-24 for a discussion of transactions versus final goods

Considering all these aspects, transactions involving final goods and service, factors of production, intermediate inputs second-hand goods and transfers, the "velocity of circulation" in the Quantity Theory equation is far removed from any measure of the actual number of times a unit of currency is exchanged in a period of time.   While it is possible that there is a fairly stable relationship between the two, it is by no means certain, especially if the composition of economic activity varies according to the state of the economy. (We might see more investment and house building in a buoyant economy, and more repairs and maintenance and trade in second-hand goods in a depressed economy.)

Methodology

10. Aggregation

Macroeconomics relies heavily on variables which are aggregates. Hence we have GDP, aggregate consumption, the price level, the labour force, a country's imports and its exports, for example. Aggregation involves the grouping together of units. It is a way to reduce the number of variables to be handled in an analysis, and it can also serve to provide an overall picture. In addition to macroeconomic aggregates, note that much of our other data is aggregated over space and time. These forms of aggregation are central to many economic models, but the result can be a serious misrepresentation of reality [see Nos. 25 and 32]. We also aggregate into individual markets, industries, types of labour, etc. Any grouping requires aggregation.

Aggregation is a form of simplification. There is no loss of information when the components of an aggregate are **homogeneous** (identical), but this requirement is rarely met. Note that homogeneity is **application-specific** in that the characteristics of the variable that are important depend on the application. An objective may be that there are jobs for all who are able and willing to work, in which case we can consider aggregate labour supply and demand. However, if the aim is to give options of high income career paths, or full-time rather than part-time work, then the type of job or hours of work are important. If export income as a whole is the point of interest, then the specific goods and services being exported may not be important. If the distribution of benefits from exports matters, then the types of exports and linkages to other industries may matter.

The homogeneity requirement can be relaxed somewhat if the **composition** of the aggregate is constant. For example, if half of your labour force is qualified and the rest unqualified, and any change in labour force is also split half and half, we could think of changes in employment as being changes in

23

the numbers of "representative workers" who are half qualified and half unqualified.

The significance of the application can be specified in further detail. It is important not only in terms of the issues being analysed, but also in terms of the functional relationships between variables. In analyses where relationships between variables are considered, homogeneity refers to the nature of this relationship. The same relationship is assumed for every component of the aggregate. In other words, the validity of an aggregate is **context-specific**. If demand for a good is unaffected by the hair colour of the individual, then aggregation over several hair colours will not change the results. If the aim is to identify the multiplier effects from increased government expenditure, it is can be important to know if the initial increased government spending is in terms of increases in domestic income or in the purchase of imports. Similarly, the increased consumption resulting from increased income may add to domestic spending for some consumers, but increased imports for others. If so, it may be important to know whose income would be increased.

You may sometimes see a mention that a particular measure has been "validated". For example, if a population sample appears to resemble the population as a whole according to chosen measures (age, ethnicity, income distribution, etc.), it might be suggested that results of analyses using those data would be valid for the country in question. This is misleading if sections of the population behave differently, because an analysis using aggregate data assumes that all components behave in the same way. Consequently validation, as with aggregation, is context-specific. Beware the rhetoric that claims otherwise.

One problem with grouping is that results are likely to reflect some form of average outcome or relationship. With the homogeneity assumption, within group variation is ignored or at least downplayed. The focus is on between-group differences. Consider income distributions for two ethnic groups. There could be a difference in average incomes of the two groups, and this might even be claimed to be important due to it being statistically significant. However, within group variation can mean that there is a big overlap in the two distributions.

Many economic models assume homogeneity of behaviour, partly because it is difficult to handle situations where there are agents who behave differently, perhaps having different objectives or information. To quote Hodgson (1997, p. 132) on modelling when there is diversity, "...it was not easy to develop a composite picture from a diversity of types of individual agent". In the real world we do observe such diversity, however. Behaviour can vary over family types, age groups, ethnicities, education levels, socio-economic groups, and so on. The same group can change its behaviour over time also, which causes further practical problems in analysis and forecasting.

11. Model building

Many economics courses and textbooks focus very heavily on models as representations of the economic phenomena under investigation. These could be considered as analogies for the real world, alternative representations which may be similar, in some respects, to the real world.[4]

An understanding of the nature of modelling can be helpful for understanding the material, especially when the texts or courses do not make this explicit. Consider the following brief outline:

1. A model in economics is constructed by specifying selected variables, some of which are **exogenous** and others which are **endogenous**.
2. The values of **exogenous** variables are set outside the model. They are not explained by the model, so their values are treated a "given".
3. The values of **endogenous** variables are set within the model according to specified relationships with the other variables, both endogenous and exogenous.
4. Note that the exogeneity of some variables is a feature of the model, not of the variables themselves. It is an assumption made by the

---

[4] I explore this issue in some detail in a SpringerBrief aimed primarily at post-graduate researchers and analysts, see Birks, 2015.

model-builder. Policy variables can be included in this category, with their values set by policy makers.

5. Some exogenous variables are not explicitly mentioned. Instead, you may see the term, *"ceteris paribus"*, a Latin expression meaning, "everything else staying the same". This means that all omitted variables are assumed to be constant. Of course, they may not be constant in reality, but we assume them to be constant in the model so as to separate out the effects of the variables of interest (this might be unrealistic, in which case the model could give misleading results).

6. Note also that the term "exogenous preferences" in the context of model construction does not mean that preferences are fixed. It just means that they are not determined within the model. Anything that might cause preferences to change (such as advertising) is beyond the scope of the model.

7. Similarly short- and long-run in relation to models are not issues of time, they relate to assumptions as to what can vary. This can be clearly seen in the theory of the firm. It is for reasons such as this that it is important to understand the process of model building and the nature of models.

8. In the initial stages, a model could be quite basic and unrealistic. A basic model "explains" very little. It commonly has few endogenous variables.

9. An economist might use this as a starting point, attempting to understand a few key characteristics.

   For a microeconomics example, consider a supply and demand model where quantities supplied and demanded depend on price alone. All other possible variables are assumed to be constant (the *ceteris paribus* assumption) or irrelevant to the relationships, but a general structure is established, including the concept of equilibrium, along with questions of its **existence, uniqueness and stability** [see No.12]. The *ceteris paribus* assumption can then be relaxed. Additional variables (consumers' incomes, prices of other goods, a sales tax) can be introduced and their effects considered. Their determinants can then be included also, or the functional relationships made more complex.

For a macroeconomics example, consider a simple circular flow diagram with no leakages or injections. Then add savings as a withdrawal and investment as an injection. Also add a government sector with taxation as a withdrawal and government expenditure on goods and services as an injection. Add government transfer payments as an additional injection (or as negative taxes). Bring in international trade with expenditure on imports as a withdrawal and income from exports as an injection. So far the interest rate and price level are assumed constant (as exogenous variables, perhaps not even mentioned). Allow the interest rate to vary, considering its effects on investment, perhaps on other aspects of expenditure, maybe international capital movements, balance of payments and exchange rates. Add a financial sector to give some explanation of interest rate determination. These are the sorts of steps you will see in a standard course.

10. As the models develop, they get more involved, giving some possible explanations for more and more phenomena. The explanations are all limited by the dimensions and specification of the model, although it may be hoped that they gradually come to more closely resemble the real world.

11. Where models are intended to aid in policy making, the design will depend in part on the policy variables being considered. A Central Bank will focus on monetary variables, interest rates and reserve ratios, for example, whereas Treasury analysts would be more concerned about the effects of fiscal variables.

12. One book which goes into some detail on the nature of models in economics is Morgan (2012).

13. As a word of caution, some economists (Lawson, 1997; Lawson, 2003) argue that these models represent "closed" systems, fully defined within the model itself, whereas the real world is a "open system" where additional outside influences may have an effect. Consequently, the models can never be realistic.

It is important to consider the constraints of a model, including its simplifying assumptions and recognising that there are additional aspects to be considered in the real world. These can be thought of in terms of the nature of framing and the processes that may be followed when analysing issues.

This perspective implicitly conveys the limited, partial nature of any approach and hence the possibility of numerous, similarly limited, alternatives.

The process of model development could be considered in terms of a series of steps:

a. make some **assumptions** (about what will be important components of the structure to be developed). These may or may not be realistic, but once they are set out, the analysis has to comply with them.[5]

b. construct a **model** based on these assumptions. A formal model involves the specification of relationships between variables.

c. (Some of the assumptions may be used to justify the relationships, but they are not then essential to the analysis. For example, a case could be made as to why a supply curve slopes upwards, but for the use of the model it is enough to require the supply curve to be upward sloping.)

d. given the model, various **conclusions** can then be determined. This requires **internal consistency** in reasoning. The model is defining the "world" in which the conclusions follow.

Significantly, there is no requirement that the conclusions be relevant for the **real world**, but they are sometimes asserted to be. Remember that a simplified structure is being used which MAY serve as a useful analogy, but it may also be highly inaccurate. There are many additional "reserves, qualifications and adjustments" that we may have to make if we are to have any confidence in the real-world relevance of the model. Hence, for example:

- static analysis does not consider adjustment paths and processes;

---

[5] Some would argue that models based on unrealistic assumptions can be of limited value for the real world, contrary to the position presented in a still very influential essay published many years ago Friedman, M. 1953. The methodology of positive economics. *In:* Friedman, M. (ed.) *Essays in positive economics.* Chicago, Ill.: University of Chicago Press. Available:
http://members.shaw.ca/compilerpress1/Anno%20Friedman%20Positive.htm.

- there is a choice as to which variables are **endogenous** (determined within the model) and which are **exogenous** (determined outside, taken as given);
- there are choices as to which variables are considered to be related to each other and where they are independent (does demand for funds vary with interest rate? Does real GDP vary with money supply?).

Some people consider that analysis of an issue should involve a choice of a theory or model, after which conclusions are those that follow from the chosen theory or model. Treating theories as analogies differs from this in two important ways. First, there may be some relevant information to be obtained from two or more theories or models, so there could be a need to somehow combine this for a more comprehensive understanding. Second, the analysis does not stop with the initial application. Additional aspects not covered by the theory or model may then have to be incorporated (such as the issue of adjustment paths and lags in adjustment, or distribution of costs and benefits of an action). Institutional or country differences may also have to be considered. This should not need to be said, but the point is frequently missed especially as the information is not always contained in quantitative data.

There is a benefit from seeing the material this way, even for those who wish only to learn the basic textbook material. It makes it clear that the findings relate to abstract models. They do not provide definitive representations of real world phenomena. The approach has the added advantage that it helps to build up critical skills and to see some processes whereby issues can be systematically analysed, along with the limitations of those processes.

12. Equilibrium, existence, uniqueness and stability

As mentioned in the discussion of static analysis above, it is an artificial construct which avoids consideration of paths through time. While we might question its relevance and hence that of equilibrium, once we agree to undertake analyses based on these concepts there are additional aspects of equilibria to consider. For a basic concept of equilibrium, as might be found in physics, or in a physics-based application to economics, think of "a system at rest" or a state of "forces in balance". When at such an equilibrium point, the same position will be maintained and there is no pressure for change unless something else changes, some other influence appears. A leaf is stationary on the ground until the wind blows it, water in a glass or vase is still until knocked, for example.

For a more specifically economic interpretation, consider a system where the agents are people. You could think of people making plans according to some expectations about their environment. Equilibrium could then be viewed as the point where "people's **plans are realised**". The actual outcome matches their expected outcome. If a system is at equilibrium, there is no incentive for change unless some determinant changes. This recognises that economic decisions are made by individuals and are based on certain expectations (such as the quantity they can buy or sell at a given price). If their plans are realised, their expectations are correct. Conversely, if they are not realised, they are likely to revise their expectations and change their behaviour, so the outcome will change.

Standard textbook descriptions of market forces suggest that those whose plans are not realised would increase the price that they are willing to pay (unsatisfied consumers under excess demand) or reduce the price that they are willing to receive (unsatisfied suppliers under excess supply). When at equilibrium, everyone's plans are realised. Nobody has an incentive to change unless a change in something else is anticipated. Out of equilibrium, plans are not realised, so, *ceteris paribus*, some participants may well change their behaviour.

This is a useful way to consider more complicated economic systems where there are several areas of activity. For example, take the Keynesian cross macroeconomic model, otherwise referred to as the 45 degree model. In this model equilibrium occurs when income equals planned expenditure (equals output, so plans are realised). In the model the interest rate is exogenous, it is determined elsewhere. If we combine it with a model of the monetary sector in which interest rates are determined, we would find that disequilibrium in the latter sector could result in a change in interest rate and subsequent changes in planned expenditure. This would result in changes in income, with repercussions on the monetary sector. The combined model may suggest a situation where there is simultaneous equilibrium in both areas. There may still be disequilibrium in labour or foreign currency markets, say, in which case further adjustments might be expected. This is the sort of thinking that underlies many static economic models.

There are some additional issues to bear in mind. With static analysis, the point of interest will be either an optimum (as with utility or profit maximisation), or an equilibrium. There are several possibilities:

- Existence – this is not guaranteed, there could be no equilibrium
- Uniqueness – if an equilibrium exists, there could be more than one equilibrium
- Stability – an equilibrium could be stable or unstable.

With a single equilibrium that is stable, if you move away from that equilibrium then adjustment pressures will result in a return to that equilibrium. With a single equilibrium that is unstable, any move away from the equilibrium will lead to further movement away from that point. With multiple equilibria, a movement away from a stable equilibrium may result in a move back to that equilibrium, or, if the initial movement is large enough, attainment of another stable equilibrium elsewhere.

Most standard supply and demand diagrams assume a single, stable equilibrium, as do many macroeconomic models. More recently, especially following the global financial crisis, some economists have focused more on behaviour out of equilibrium and away from models which rely on stable equilibria. Economists with more of a historical and institutional focus are less willing to view the world according to static models. They are more concerned with process and paths of change over time.

13. *Ceteris paribus* assumptions

Given the complexity of real world economic activity, any model can at best be only a partial representation of reality. Inevitably, some things are omitted. There is a necessary assumption that these things are either constant or irrelevant. The *ceteris paribus* assumption is that all omitted variables are constant and consequently there are no changes in these variables that might affect the working of the model.

While the assumption is in practice automatically made, the real world relevance of a model depends in part on whether the assumption is legitimate. Consider the assumption in a macroeconomic context where price changes occur "ceteris paribus". To quote Omkarnath (2012, p. 74) "An increase in the price of commodities, howsoever brought about, must mean an increase in incomes somewhere in the economy." Similarly in microeconomics it is often assumed that a market can be considered in isolation. Under this assumption changes in the market in question will not change prices in other related markets, such as markets for substitutes or complements. If they do change other relevant prices, there would be feedback effects to consider. Increased demand for university places brings increased demand for student accommodation, which raises the price of student accommodation, which reduces demand for student places. Sometimes the effects are just in terms of available income. Increases in student fees reduce student net income and this limits spending on food.

This indicates that *ceteris paribus* assumptions, while essential for reducing the complexity of a model and allowing manageable analysis, may result in important aspects being overlooked. More traditional attempts to analyse an economic issue would rely heavily on observation, introspection, exploration of possibilities, and then perhaps some more formal modelling. It is when the models are the starting point that serious, unidentified errors and misrepresentations are most likely to occur.

A related problem can arise when we consider the use of observations for quantitative analysis. Consider a situation where there are observations of both tight and loose monetary policy and also of both tight and loose fiscal policy (assuming the policies are each simple enough to be defined in this one-dimensional way). Imagine that these observations are such that whenever there is tight monetary policy there is also tight fiscal policy, and whenever there is loose monetary policy there is also loose fiscal policy. While it might be thought that the whole range of monetary and fiscal policy options are covered, the data cannot be assumed to demonstrate the effects of a policy mix where one is tight and the other is loose. Moreover, and to stress the *ceteris paribus* point here, there is no set of observations that can be used to show one policy changing while the other stays constant. If we have never observed the situation, it is hard to argue that the data can describe what would happen. However, this is what the *ceteris paribus* assumption requires. (For another twist on this point, see active versus accommodating monetary policy in No.24.)

With only two variables as in the above example, it may be possible to check the combinations covered, although this check may not be undertaken. More complex models have many variables, so it is much harder to see which combined possibilities have been observed and which have not.

A parallel can be drawn with the use of "control variables" in econometrics, where it is often claimed that, by means of these variables, certain phenomena have been "controlled for". If variables impact on each other so that the effects of one cannot be singled out and removed, then the process results in misrepresentation and questionable results.

Simplification in microeconomics assumes that a chosen phenomenon, such as a specific market, firm or consumer, can be analysed in isolation. In macroeconomics simplification emphasises a much higher degree of aggregation. There is a term to describe an intermediate level of analysis, although such analyses are seldom observed. Mesoeconomics relates to situations where smaller scale (microeconomic) changes can affect an economy as a whole (macroeconomic). For example, a major financial institution or dominant industry can be large enough for its activities to have a macroeconomic impact. While there is not much written on this area, some situations may be better suited to analysis of this form.

14. Long run and short run

Note from the discussion of model building [No.11] that short run and long run relate to assumptions as to what can vary. With production, some inputs are assumed to be fixed in the short run, whereas all inputs can be varied in the long run. Short-run or long-run effects are defined in this context. Note that this is not a matter of actual length of time required. It is simply the terminology used to distinguish between two theoretical representations. We could consider the commonly presented short-run situation where capital is fixed and labour is allowed to vary. Alternatively labour could be assumed fixed and capital allowed to vary. The approaches are really attempting to address the problem, if X is fixed, how to we optimise with respect to Y.

With demand or supply curves the short run and long run are less clearly distinguishable. There is a general presumption that more options are available in the longer run, permitting larger responses in terms of quantities demanded or supplied. This is the basis for the claim that demand and supply are more elastic in the long run than in the short run.

In macroeconomics we also come across the long run and the short run. Again the distinction is one of ability to adjust. In reality economic activity is defined in terms of "flow variables", income per year, consumption per year, etc. This differs from static analysis in that adjustments may not have time to work themselves out before some other change occurs. Textbooks today commonly describe the long-run macroeconomic situation as one of equilibrium at full employment, whereas the economy can deviate from this full employment situation in the short run.

We only have data which (perhaps imperfectly) indicates actual situations. When describing graphs of macroeconomic aggregate income data a story is often told of a long-run trend and short-run fluctuations around that trend. This is very convenient for story-telling because it suggests that the two, long-run and short-run, can be considered separately. However, short-run fluctuations affect investment and employment, which influence the age and composition of the capital stock and the skills and experience of the labour force (note the term "human capital"). These affect the size and quality of capital and labour, this affecting potential output and hence long-run trends. Short-run fluctuations can have long-run implications.

In microeconomics also, there are points to note about the distinction between short and long run. Much is made of the value of price signals for resource allocation decisions.

In estimating the relationships specified by this framing, we are reliant on the same data for both situations. The data may not accurately reflect either of these, and it could be wondered how the same data could be used to estimate both short-run and long-run relationships.[6] This can be illustrated by the example of electricity prices. In the short run it is desirable to optimally use existing generating capacity. Given that the marginal cost of generation can be low when there is spare capacity (think of hydroelectricity) it is desirable to set a low price for current consumption.[7] However, people will also be making decisions on the type of power to use for factories, home heating, etc. (demand being more flexible in the long run). If a prevailing low price of electricity is used as a basis for these investment decisions, there will be an increase in the number of electricity-powered factories and home heating systems. The resulting increased demand for electricity may take up all the excess capacity and result in a requirement for additional capacity at much higher cost. In other words, in this example the short-run marginal cost of electricity is low, but the long-run marginal cost is high. If price reflects the former, it is good for current consumption of electricity, but sends the wrong signal for investment decisions that affect future electricity demand.

The distinction between the long run and the short run can be helpful for systematic analysis, but it comes at a cost. It misrepresents the phenomena that we are trying to analyse and, at the empirical stage, it requires us to make unrealistic assumptions about the data and the relationships that we wish to observe.

15. Proof and consistency

In his essay "The methodology of positive economics" Friedman wrote:

> "Observed facts are necessarily finite in number; possible
> hypotheses, infinite. If there is one hypothesis that is

---

[6] The meaning of short run and long run in economics may also differ from that used in econometrics.
[7] There may be **natural monopoly** characteristics to the supply of electricity, with implications for pricing structures.

consistent with the available evidence, there are always an
infinite number that are" (Friedman, 1953, p. 9).

He makes an important point. It is not possible to prove a theory by
observing the real world. All that can be deduced, at best, is that the theory
is not contradicted by the evidence. In other words the evidence is
consistent with the theory. The evidence may contradict the theory, in
which case we know that, at the very least, the theory is not universally
applicable. There is at least one situation where the theory did not apply.
Where the theory is not contradicted this may be because the theory gives
the real explanation of the phenomenon, but there will be other possible
explanations, and one or more of these may be more valid. For example,
there may be a statistical association between lung cancer deaths and
cigarette lighters in the home. This is consistent with a hypothesis that
cigarette lighters cause lung cancer, but, as you no doubt realise, it is also
consistent with smoking causing lung cancer.

This is important when there is debate between alternative schools of
thought. It may be possible to give explanations of many types of behaviour
using a particular body of theory, such as that based on utility maximising
individuals. This could give *an* explanation, but it is not necessarily *the*
explanation, especially if individuals operate in other ways. For example, you
may come across "satisficing" behaviour, whereby people are not always
trying to do the best, but instead just doing enough, or alternatively they may
be acting according to habit, or social convention, of by applying simple
heuristics. Consequently, an investigator should recognise the there is more
to be done than simply find an explanation that is consistent with that body
of thought, unless, of course, the objective is simply one of defending a
preferred perspective.

Use of evidence

We can go a step further. To find consistency requires both theory and
evidence. These two are combined along with some type of test whereby if
the evidence meets certain criteria it is judged to be consistent, otherwise it
would be inconsistent, or perhaps the conclusion is indeterminate. We
should not overlook the crucial importance of the test, therefore.

Economics research commonly relies heavily on quantitative techniques (using numerical data), whereas qualitative research, which may use interview, textual and other data, is more frequently used in other social sciences. It should be recognised that a broad definition of data includes all forms of information which may be useful for increasing our understanding. It can be helpful to make a comparison with history. Econometric data describe situations that have already occurred. Analysis of these data is therefore a form of historical analysis. When compared to the rich variety of sources and methods used by historians, econometrics implicitly excludes much of this information from the analysis. Rather than treating this restriction as a starting and unstated assumption, we could (and should) ask ourselves whether we can justify not using these data. Of course, these additional data (reports, policy documents, speeches, images, etc.) may have to be analysed using other techniques.

Carr (2008 [1961]) described one of the actions of a historian as looking at the available information and deciding what, out of all that is available, will be selected as "the facts". The basic units of information that we use for analysis are selected, and this is part of the process of framing. To some extent our choices are limited. Numerical data, such as those on output, employment, income and industries, are collected by other people for other purposes. We must then work with what is available. We should still be aware of the meaning and limitations of these data.

We can then analyse the information to draw conclusions. The process generally involves specifying a hypothesis and a criterion on which to test the hypothesis. **The result depends on both the actual situation and the nature of the test.**

False positives and false negatives

A test may not be fool-proof. For example, there could be **false positives** or **false negatives**. If a positive result equates to consistency and a negative result to inconsistency, then a false positive result occurs then the test indicates consistency when, in reality, the theory is inconsistent. Conversely a false negative arises when the test incorrectly suggests inconsistency. We see these terms used in the health area relation to tests for cancer, say. A false positive would indicate the presence of cancer when the subject is cancer free, and a false negative would give a negative result (no cancer) when cancer is actually present.

Ex ante and ex post

There is an additional dimension in the application of theory to observed events. The term **ex ante** refers to before an event, and **ex post** refers to after an event. It is relatively easy to take an observed event and then fit a theoretical explanation to it, *ex post*. It is much harder to take a theory *ex ante* and accurately predict an event that occurs subsequently.

There are daily TV and radio reports of share price movements on stock exchanges. These commonly mention a price change and then give an explanation (*ex post*). For example, if prices have been rising for some days and then fall, this could be explained in terms of investors "profit taking". If an event occurs and a share price changes, it could be explained as the market responding to the news. If, instead, the price does not change, the explanation could be that "the market had already taken the news into account". The question is whether these are explanations or rationalisations. We cannot tell unless an explanation is given in advance of the event (*ex ante*), such that it is selecting from all the possible responses to give a prediction of a future outcome. It is much easier, but far less meaningful, to give consistent explanations *ex post* than it is *ex ante*.

In summary, the link from theory and hypotheses via data analyses to the real world is not clear cut. This limits the confidence with which we can make statements about the real world.

16. The Theory of Second Best

The Theory of Second Best is potentially a major spoiler in the application of economic theory to the real world. A classic article on this theory is Lipsey and Lancaster (1956). Put simply, it says that a finding that holds in theory when all the assumptions of the theory are met may be of little value for other situations where one of more of the assumptions is not met.

Keen (2011) gives a good illustration based on the desirability of a perfectly competitive economy. Consider a situation where there are monopolies, which are the sole hirers of certain types pf worker (i.e. they are monopsonistic hirers of labour) and unions (which are monopolistic suppliers of labour). He asks if you would abolish one of these if the other would still exist. Arguably, that could lead to a worse outcome than if both existed.

If you are familiar with the mathematics of constrained optimisation, the nature of the problem can be readily explained. You will know that the addition of a new constraint changes the optimal conditions. This can give two ways to think of the theory. Consider the option of a policy to remove a constraint, X, that goes against the conditions for perfect competition (i.e. a market failure):

1. If there is another, additional constraint, Y, that cannot be removed, then other optimal conditions may no longer be appropriate. Consequently it may not be desirable to remove constraint X. Alternatively,
2. If there are many constraints preventing perfect competition (say), then the optimal conditions are likely to be quite different from those under perfect competition. Removal or reduction of some constraints may not give an improvement.

In practice, there are many breaches of the overall conditions for perfect competition. For example, we do not live in a static world of utility maximising atomistic (separate and independent) individuals where resources are all allocated by markets under perfect information and well-defined property rights. The Theory of Second Best indicates that policies to correct for some selected market failure defined in relation to such a perfectly competitive world will not necessarily result in an improvement overall. Put another way, the real world is far more complex than a simple model with one market failure. We should not just assume that the latter accurately describes the former.

The Theory of Second Best really indicates that the findings of economic theory are unlikely to be directly applicable to the real world. It is a **fatal flaw**

in the application of theory. The real world does not operate according to all the assumptions of economic theory. Even if, as some imagine, theoretical findings are indicative of the real world situation, additional thought is needed to consider the importance of deviations from the theory. It may be that such consideration cannot be done through formal analysis (otherwise it could be modelled and the problem would not arise).

There is a similar "fatal flaw" in econometrics. There is a term, "omitted variable bias", whereby omission of a relevant variable (or misspecification of the functional form) results in biased estimates of the model. However, any model involves simplification in the selection of variables (hopefully choosing the most important ones) and in the choice of functional form (linear, etc.). Inevitably, some relevant variables will be omitted.

17. Framing

As a general rule, it is useful to be aware of the importance of **framing**. The process of framing refers to the way in which things are observed. It applies to any description or analysis, not just within economics. Framing has been described as involving **selection, emphasis, exclusion and elaboration**. It is particularly important to note what is included and what is excluded. Framing shapes what we see, the problems that are identified and the policy suggestions that result. Society has been viewed in many different ways, with each framing giving a different picture. We could focus on economic, political or social dimensions. We could consider a society divided into classes, or ethnic groups, or by gender. The distribution of income and wealth would come across differently according to the groupings we select. History could be presented in terms of, for example, i) kings and queens, and dates of battles and wars, or ii) the lives of common people. Activity could be divided into public or private; market or non-market; work or leisure; employer, self-employed, employee; and so on.

Carr (2008 [1961]), in a series of lectures on history presented in 1961, said that the historian did not look at the facts and draw conclusions. The historian selected from all the available information, deciding what to take as the facts, then using these to present an interpretation. The historian selected some information, emphasised some points over others, and told a story by elaborating on these, while ignoring or excluding other information.

Historians are not the only ones to work in this way. Frequently, within a discipline, the framing is largely determined by prevailing conventions. Mainstream microeconomics emphasises markets and market failure, the role of prices, and rational individuals maximising profit or utility. Similarly macroeconomics uses standard components of aggregate expenditure and considers economic problems such as inflation, unemployment, and growth in overall output. Other branches of economics, often referred to as heterodox (in contrast to orthodox) economics, along with more inclusive pluralist perspectives, challenge some of these conventions. In particular, a common criticism is that mainstream economics is too abstract and based on unrealistic assumptions or postulates. The focus on scarcity as a central concern of economics has also been questioned. It has been argued that in some societies, scarcity is generated through promotion of demand, as with some advertising, or with "planned obsolescence".

18. Consequentialism

Put simply, consequentialism could be described as "the ends justify the means". The focus is on the end result where the best choice is the option which gives the best outcome. Examples in economics would include optimisation problems such as profit maximisation or utility maximisation. This is why an awareness of consequentialism is important. It emphasises that we may, in the real world, also be concerned about the means. Rather than just being concerned about the outcome that we achieve, we may also be concerned about how we achieve that outcome.

Note that an outcome such as an optimum point is a static concept [see No.2]. That is not the world in which we live. We are permanently on a journey through time. Where we are now is a point on the way to where we will be tomorrow, and the next day. How we got somewhere is also where we were yesterday. What we do today affects where we will be, or could be, tomorrow. The structures or processes that we follow also provide our lived experiences. A focus on static analysis suggests that some mythical end result should be the sole focus. It is implicitly assumed that this endpoint might be attained and sustained for a long time, whereas the journey there is just a short-term transient state that can be ignored.

A more historical perception of time might suggest that many things are changing. We are always adjusting and adapting, making mistakes, reversing directions, facing the unexpected and, through all this, living our lives.

Theoretical analyses are inevitably simplifications. Consequentialism highlights one form of simplification inherent in conventional mainstream economics.

19. Pareto optimality and cost-benefit analysis

How do we decide if a situation is optimal? How can we determine if a change is beneficial? This is important if we are to evaluate policy options. Welfare economics has attempted to provide criteria on which to base policy decisions.

A starting point for this is individual utility. That is not the only option, but it follows naturally from the atomistic foundation of mainstream microeconomics based on separate, independent individuals. If this (conceptual) measure can be used for individual decision making, perhaps it may serve as a basis for comparing outcomes for society.

Also utility is now commonly considered as an **ordinal**, rather than a **cardinal** measure. It may be possible to identify whether an individual prefers A over B, but not the amount of utility gained from either A or B, or the difference in utilities. If there is no acceptable fixed, cardinal measure, then it is also not possible to compare utility gained by different individuals. In other words, **interpersonal comparison of utility** is not possible.

If we only have ordinal utility with no interpersonal comparison, we are limited in our ability to compare situations. This is where the Pareto criterion comes in. A change whereby one or more people become better off (obtain higher utility) and nobody is worse off (gets lower utility) is a **Pareto improvement**.

From a given starting point it may be possible to achieve a Pareto improvement, and further improvements may be possible from there. At some stage a point will be reached from which on individual can gain without someone else losing. Such a point is **Pareto Optimal** or **Pareto Efficient**.

A key finding in economics, the **First Fundamental Theorem of Welfare Economics**, states that an economy in perfectly competitive equilibrium is Pareto Optimal. Among other things, this has been taken to show that, at least conceptually, it is possible to have an economy where everyone is pursuing their own self-interest and the result is in one sense "best" for society as a whole. Sen (1977) pointed out that this was demonstrated as an intellectual exercise. The circumstances are far from realistic, but the finding has come to have great real world significance as a justification for reliance on markets.

Note that:
    i)   Pareto Optimal situations may arise independently of markets, so, while perfect competition implies Pareto Optimality, the reverse does not hold (Pareto Optimality does not imply perfect competition).
    ii)   a static optimum may not be most desirable given the importance of changes over time;
    iii) there may be Pareto Optimal situations that we consider highly undesirable (such as those in which some people are living in abject poverty); and
    iv) we may place value not simply on outcomes, but also on the way outcomes are achieved (see "consequentialism").

Many policy and other changes can result in some people gaining and others losing. Such changes cannot be seen as a Pareto Improvement, so the principle does not give any guidance as to what decision to make. To assist in such cases, the **compensation criterion** suggests that a change is beneficial if the gainers can compensate the losers and still be better off. If the compensation is actually paid, then the result of the combined change plus compensation would be a Pareto Improvement.

There is an important qualification, however. Under the compensation criterion the compensation does not have to be paid. You might consider this to be unsatisfactory. If so, then it indicates a problem with a common form of economic evaluation. **Cost-benefit analysis** (CBA) is widely used in an attempt to assess the merits of projects or policy changes. Costs and benefits are identified and evaluated, after which a decision rule could be applied to determine or recommend a course of action. In simple cases a decision rule that can be applied in CBA is that benefits should outweigh costs. There is no consideration of the allocation of benefits and costs. In other words, **the use of this rule implies adoption of the compensation criterion**. One challenge that could be made to a CBA decision would then be to question its redistributive implications, asking who is gaining, who is losing and by how much. More conventionally, the rule is applied without this qualification.

20. Externalities and the "Coase Theorem"

Market failures can be seen as a reason for government intervention. The failure is in comparison to the "ideal" of perfect competition. We may not wish to use this as a basis for comparison, given that, i) it may be unattainable, and ii) it may not be the optimal for society anyway. These are important qualifications, but textbook analyses generally follow this format.

Externalities arise when a market transaction results in costs or benefits to others who are not a party to the transaction. Consequently, in the standard representation, the supply and demand curve are considered to represent only private marginal costs and benefits, and these differ from the social marginal costs and benefits (which also consider costs and benefits to these other affected people). This is easy to illustrate in a supply and demand diagram by drawing alternative curves to represent the social rather than the private position. A commonly suggested solution to the problem is then to impose a per unit tax (for an external cost) or subsidy (for an external benefit) such that the equilibrium after the tax or subsidy coincides with the socially desirable equilibrium. The required condition in such a model is that the tax or subsidy per unit reflects the marginal external cost or benefit at this new equilibrium point. It all looks very tidy and some will suggest that it gives an optimal solution, or solves the problem. As an alternative e description, it could be said that the externality has been "internalised". The costs or benefits are now reflected in the production/pricing/consumption decision. In reality it is not so straight forward:

i)   there may be measurement problems,
ii) even if a tax is used to alter the price, thereby taking into account external costs, it does not mean that those who suffer the external cost receive any of the tax revenue (and similarly no payment is required from those receiving external benefits).

It may be possible to do something about the first problem, but the second will still remain. Costs or benefits are addressed by additional transactions with the government, but that is not the party affected by the costs or benefits.

The Coase Theorem gives a different perspective. It is used to argue that, if property rights have been allocated (a factory has a right to pollute, or neighbouring households have a right not to face pollution), then the people causing and affected by an externality can negotiate to reach an efficient solution. This is irrespective of which party is given the rights. If there is value from the polluting activity but households have the right not to face pollution, the factory could pay the households in exchange for their permission to pollute. If the factory has the right to pollute, but the costs are high enough, households could pay the factory in exchange for its limiting the pollution.

It is a strange interpretation of the original analysis. Coase (1991), in his Nobel acceptance lecture, spoke of:

"...the infamous Coase Theorem, named and formulated by Stigler, although it is based on work of mine. Stigler argues that the Coase Theorem follows from the standard assumptions of economic theory. Its logic cannot be questioned, only its domain. I do not disagree with Stigler. However, I tend to regard the Coase Theorem as a stepping stone on the way to an analysis of an economy with positive transaction costs."

In other words, Coase was saying not that an optimal outcome could be achieved through negotiation, but rather that the required negotiation may not happen, or would at least be costly. It is not enough for legislation or the courts simply to allocate property rights in any way they choose, after which some "invisible hand" will guarantee a satisfactory outcome. Time consuming and costly legal deliberation may occur, and it is not always clear what the outcome will then be.

Policy

21. Fixed targets

One approach to modelling an economic policy problem is to have one set of variables as the policy targets (inflation, unemployment, etc.), another set of variables as policy instruments (government expenditure, money supply), and specified relationships between them. Tinbergen (1952), using mathematical representations of the problem, made the point that it is possible to achieve an outcome specified in terms of fixed targets (specific values for the target variables) if there are as many policy instruments as independent target variables. The finding is well known and results from the requirements for solving a set of equations.

Tinbergen does elaborate on some mathematical requirements, but this is often omitted in general descriptions of the approach. The finding breaks down once we have more complex relationships or consider costs of policies. This highlights the danger of transplanting simple theoretical results as if they apply to real world situations.

To express two basic points, first, while it may be possible to achieve any configuration of target variables with an equal number of policy instruments, additional assumptions are needed, such as that no two instruments have identical effects, there are no bounds on the feasible application of the instruments (e.g. are negative interest rates possible?), and there are no limits to their impacts on the target variables (e.g. Laffer curve effects limiting tax revenue[8]).

---

[8] The Laffer curve reflects the fact that a zero tax rate will give zero revenue, as would a very high tax rate (imagine income tax at 100% of income!), but that tax rates between these extremes will yield positive revenue. There is therefore some rate that will maximise revenue, beyond which higher tax rates will result in falling revenue. Some collective communities may effectively have 100% tax rates if all

Second, nothing is said about the costs of attainment of a configuration. That is not part of the specified objective. Fixed targets are to be achieved irrespective of cost. All Tinbergen's point gives us is a necessary, but not sufficient, condition for attainment of fixed targets, with no consideration of optimality. This may be of limited relevance. We are unlikely to rely heavily on fixed targets and the minimum required number of instruments as they are associated with a highly simplified representation of the environment. When would we choose such an objective (other than for inflation targeting with a single monetary policy instrument)?

22. Flexible targets and policy evaluation

Policy making based on a model with fixed targets and an equal number of instruments can give a unique solution in terms of policy settings, but this is only because many of the issues of concern for policy making have been predetermined. The targets have been chosen, so there is no need to choose between alternative policy options and, if the mathematical requirements are met, there are no trade-offs required as all targets can be simultaneously achieved.

Real world policy making is more complex. Instead of wanting a set level of inflation, the aim may be to achieve low inflation while also having regard for unemployment and growth, or it may be desirable to encourage innovation (as with patents), but also to encourage competition (which, at least in the short run, is reduced by patents). Consequently, if there is to be an assessment of the desirability of a policy, some form of policy evaluation is required so that alternative options can be compared. This commonly involves a (formal or informal) assessment of costs and benefits.

Models can suggest possible outcomes of policies, subject to their assumptions and estimated parameters. These may bear some relation to the real world outcomes which would be observed, but they may not

---

revenue is centrally reallocated independently of the contribution made. This was common in Israeli kibbutzim until reforms introduced from late 1990s. Tax revenue would then be positive, but not necessarily as high as where there is income retained income.

describe the adjustment paths and processes, and they will not generally give measures of the costs and benefits of predicted changes. Also, a model may not indicate all of the alternative policy options available. Consequently, comparisons over options may require additional information from other models or elsewhere.

It is worth noting the Maslow's well known statement, "I suppose it is tempting, if the only tool you have is a hammer, to treat everything as if it were a nail" (Maslow, 1966, pp. 15-16).

Decisions have to be made on the costs and benefits to be measured. Some elementary questions would be required for even a basic assessment. What aspects are important? By how much do they change as a result of a policy? What value might we place on this change? Even these questions may be difficult to answer with any accuracy. A more complex assessment would involve consideration of different scales of policy (the amount of a tax or interest change, for example), and comparison with alternative policy options (including the *status quo* or do nothing option). Common approaches to policy evaluation such as cost-benefit analysis (CBA) provide a single figure evaluation for each alternative plus a decision rule for choosing over the alternatives (which may be as simple as two options, proceed or not proceed). There are limitations to this also [see the compensation criterion in No.19.

23. Aims, goals and objectives

Economic models can be applied to policy questions by including variables that represent policy objectives or targets (such as growth rates), variables that represent policy instruments (such as tax rates), and relationships between them. This can be helpful for identifying policy options, but it has several limitations. One area for additional consideration is the choice of objectives.

A structure that I encountered in planning can be helpful here. It is based on the concept of a hierarchy of plans where the component plans have different levels of generality, time horizon and detail. For example, there could be three tier planning structure including long-, medium- and short-term plans. A broad plan might have a 20-year time horizon and indicate general directions and long-term aims. A somewhat more detailed plan with a 5-year time horizon could specify what is to be achieved in that period on the way to fulfilling the 20-year plan. A 1-year plan could then specify in some detail the steps to be taken immediately so as to fulfil the 5-year plan. There could of course be many more tiers, with several plans at any one tier.

To simplify the discussion and to emphasise a specific point, it can be helpful to consider the terminology of "aims, goals and objectives". Taking the structure above, instead of saying that each plan has objectives, we could say that the long-term plan has aims, the medium term plan has goals and the short-term plan has objectives. These require measures or indicators. Aims could be in terms of improving wellbeing or quality of life. Goals could be in terms of immunisation rates or education standards. Objectives could refer to smaller changes in these measures or steps on the way to achieving them, such as an immunisation campaign in an area or a reduction in school drop-out rates compared to the previous year.

Note that attention is often given to measures of objectives. These are frequently more specific than aims or goals, and new results come out more frequently. Consequently they are likely to have most impact on behaviour as people compete to achieve good results. In recent years there has been a proliferation of such measures, often under the label, "KPIs", or key performance indicators.

A danger arising from this approach is that actions to meet objectives may in fact be detrimental to the attainment of goals or aims. One example was a country that wanted to increase its international competitiveness. To do this, it set itself an objective of low inflation. Monetary policies to reduce inflation led to high interest rates, giving reduced investment in plant and machinery. They also led to capital inflows and a higher exchange rate which generated adverse effects on the traded goods sectors. More generally, there is always the possibility of **'perverse incentives'** and **'unanticipated consequences'**.

Related issues can be observed in relations to policy application and incentives. Measures identified under objectives are frequently the ones used for performance measurement. This raises issues of **perverse incentives, ticking boxes**, or **data manipulation**. Once a variable becomes important for policy or for penalties and rewards there are incentives to focus on the measure rather than the wider goals or aims.

Students will be aware of this when they focus on course assessment instead of acquisition of knowledge. The aim of education provision is to develop knowledge and critical thinking skills. The goal of a degree is to move towards the aims through a combination of relevant and increasingly demanding areas of study. The objectives of an individual paper are to contribute specific aspects of knowledge and skill. Assessment is partly a component of the learning process, but significantly it is an attempt to determine whether a student has satisfactorily achieved the objectives. It may be possible to get the required marks through cramming the night before a test, question spotting, loose paraphrasing from Wikipedia or elsewhere, or rote learning, while not achieving the goals and objectives of a qualification. This may demonstrate the possession of some other skills, but you might not want to pay for the services of a doctor or other professional who had shown that particular ability. This can be a problem with any evaluation measure, with heavy focus on the listed measures rather than on the broader concerns that the evaluation is intended to assess.

24. Forecasting

We only have information about the past, but policies only affect the future, so we have to use the former to assist us with the latter. Forecasting involves using the available information from the past to estimate the situation at some time or times in the future. This requires a degree of structural stability in the relationships, but this may not always be experienced. Some things change only slowly. Hence next month's unemployment numbers may be very similar to the numbers for this month. However, other things can change very rapidly. A share market may experience steady growth for some time, but this may result in a bubble which eventually bursts and share prices may suddenly collapse. Even if such a collapse can be anticipated, the exact timing may still be uncertain. More generally trends, and continuing trends, are relatively easy to forecast, but turning points or sharp changes in direction are not.

Economic behaviour is the combined result of decisions by many people, and people may choose to behave in various ways under the same circumstances. In some instances behaviour will differ when the same conditions are repeated. Note the example of plans not being realised. If people respond in one way on one occasion and the outcomes are not as anticipated, they are likely to respond differently the next time. While learning from experience is likely for any specific group of decision makers, it cannot be assumed for an economy over time. Decision makers change, people are replaced due to age, past performance and other reasons, and a new generation of decision makers may then repeat the mistakes of the past.

Lucas (1976), in what has come to be termed **"the Lucas critique"**, argued that data from before a policy change cannot be used to predict behaviour after the change because behaviour may well also change given the different environment. This is particularly important if the new policy environment has not existed before. The same could be said of institutional change, and institutions defined in a broad sense include general beliefs and conventions, many of which are constantly changing (consider differences in values of different generations). It may then be that there is no evidence as to how the economy might respond. If, as has happened in the past in many countries, an economy operated only under a fixed exchange rate regime, or had fixed, regulated interest rates, then it could be difficult to know how the economy would respond if the exchange rate or interest rates were allowed to vary. Similarly, if monetary and fiscal policies had always moved together, each only being restrictive or expansionary if the other is also, then i) it is difficult to separate the effects of each policy and ii) there is no evidence on outcomes if they were to operate under opposing settings, one expansionary and the other restrictive.

The effects of policy changes may differ for other reasons, such as the circumstances under which the policy change is introduced. Consider two different environments under which there could be an increase in money supply. It may be decided that there would be an accommodating monetary policy, in which case increases in the price level result in increased demand for money, after which the monetary authorities allow expansion in money supply to accommodate this increased demand. Alternatively there could be an active monetary policy where money supply changes are made to bring about changes in economic activity. In this case monetary expansion would occur if it is felt that demand is too low and some economic stimulus is required. These are very different situations under which money supply might be expected to relate very differently to other economic aggregates. Note, for example, that price level changes might lead money supply changes in the former situation, but follow them with a lag in the latter. Analyses of past data may not distinguish between these situations, in which case a single relationship would be estimated with potentially misleading results.

There is a further complicating factor in that the effects of a policy change have to be judged in relation to an unobserved counterfactual, what would have happened otherwise. Quantitative analyses tend to consider only the observed outcomes, thus sometimes providing perverse results. A fully effective price level stabilisation policy resulting in no fluctuations in price level could give a statistical result that money supply changes appear to have no effect on the price level.

The importance of forecasts and the precision required depends on the objectives to be achieved and the sophistication of the policy instruments available. So called "fine-tuning" of an economy refers to a high level of control over outcomes. This is very demanding and requires both very accurate forecasts and clinical policy instruments. For both these dimensions the concept of lags is important.

25. Lags

Static analysis ignores the time dimension. In reality it takes time to make and then apply policies, so we are only able to affect the future. Sometimes the time required from initial planning to obtaining the final outcome is quite short, as when an individual decides to make a cup of coffee, or flights are cancelled due to fog, but more often there are long delays, as in deciding to study for a degree, or to build a new airport. Ideally we would like to have policies for which the effects are felt very quickly, with no later repercussions. Consider Figure 5 where the vertical axis measures proportion of desired policy impact and the horizontal axis measures time from the introduction of a policy.

Figure 5

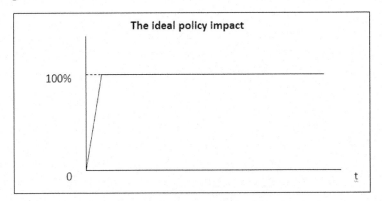

In practice, there can be initial delays before a policy is even implemented, and after that there are many time paths could be considered for the impact of the policy. Some of these are indicated in Figure 6.

Figure 6

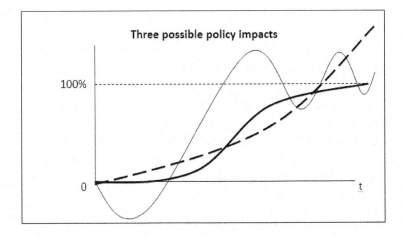

The heavy solid line indicates a policy which takes some time before much impact is felt, after which things speed up, with the final effects then coming through relatively slowly and eventually tail off. The dotted line suggests an unstable policy which might initially have a fairly slow impact, but eventually overshoot the desired target, requiring later corrective action. The thin solid line shows a cyclical pattern of impact, initially worsening the situation and then overshooting before fluctuating around and gradually converging to the target level. The case of livestock can be used to illustrate the initial negative effect. Consider an increased demand for beef. Animals can be used for beef production or for breeding stock to produce next season's beef. The price of beef rises and farmers wish to increase their stock numbers. More animals are retained for breeding and so, initially, fewer animals are available for beef production.

These are just three of many possible alternative paths that might be observed. Moreover, the path of impact of a policy on one application may differ from that on another. For some, repeated application may become less effective as people become accustomed to them or find ways to protect themselves from them (as with tax avoidance), whereas others may become more effective as institutions and conventions develop (as with anti-smoking measures).

The diagrams above consider the time after the implementation of a policy. One useful classification of lags[9] refers to this as the **outside lag**. The same classification also identifies an **inside lag**, the time required before implementation can begin.

The inside lag can be quite lengthy. First it is necessary to identify that an issue may require attention (an **observation lag**). Some variables, such as exchange rates, are regularly monitored, whereas others, such as climate change, may only be initially recognised after some decades. There is then time required to decide what policy response, if any, to make (a **decision lag**). This could involve analysis and then a decision by one individual, or complex political debate, public consultation, international negotiation, etc.. Once decided, implementation may not be immediately possible. There may

---

[9] See Chapter 10 section 4 of Vane and Thompson Vane, H. R. & Thompson, J. L. 1993. *An introduction to macroeconomic policy*. New York, Harvester Wheatsheaf..

be an **administration lag**. New construction may involve planning and design, purchase of land, tendering for required materials and so on. Tax changes may require altered paper work, accounting software, staff training, etc.. An expansionary fiscal policy through increased expenditure on final goods and services requires decisions on the specific spending that will be undertaken. Increased public sector employment requires the specification of positions to be filled, advertising and calling for applicants and then further delays before the people start work.

There are therefore many reasons why policies cannot be introduced instantaneously and their effects felt immediately. This time dimension is an important factor when determining the influence that policy or decision makers may have.

26. Equity

One of the frequently mentioned criteria for determining the desirability of a policy is that of equity. The terms "fair" and "equitable' are often used interchangeably, but without explanation as to their meaning. They are "feel-good" words, who could object to a policy suggestion that would promote equity? What does it mean, though? How can we determine if something is equitable?

Economists attempting to address this issue have provided some insights. However, if anything this has simply served to show that there is no clear answer. If you hear someone confidently claiming that their proposal should be supported on equity grounds, you can be reasonably confident that they do not really know what it means.

What economists found? There are two broad approaches that economists have used, one using concepts of **horizontal and vertical equity** and another using the **benefit principle**.

Horizontal and vertical equity

A common distinction is that between horizontal and vertical equity. **Horizontal equity** requires equal treatment under equal circumstances. **Vertical equity** requires an appropriate difference in treatment under different circumstances. While simple in concept these are both very complicated in practice.

Horizontal equity
To start with the easiest, consider horizontal equity. The first step is to determine what, or whom, we are discussing. Equal treatment of what? What are the basic units for comparison? They could be individuals, couples, households, families, businesses, or some other entity.

Having decided on the units, we then have to determine what is meant by "equal circumstances". This could overcome some of the problems caused by the distinctions above. Hence, if our starting point is the individual, then requiring an equal number of dependents would be similar to an analysis based on families with a requirement of similar family composition. Such a requirement can have heavy data requirements, though, and we should probably have simply started with data on families. Data are generally collected either for individuals or for households, with families being defined as specific household types. This means that all the members of a family are assumed to live all the time in the same household. From that starting point there will be households of differing composition as to number and ages of members. Adjustments can then be made to standardise these data using "household equivalence scales". These provide adjustment factors recognising the possibilities of economies of scale so that, for example, a two adult household might be considered to require 50% more income than a one adult household to be on the same living standard, whereas a two adult and one child household might require 80% more income.[10] More complex adjustments might consider equivalent costs being dependent on the ages of children.

---

[10] Data from the OECD-modified scale as at: http://www.oecd.org/eco/growth/OECD-Note-EquivalenceScales.pdf

There are numerous other dimensions to consider, however. Should we consider income as the variable for comparison, so that equal income is required? If so, do we take weekly income or annual income, for example? What of those with seasonal income, or those (such as farmers) whose income can vary greatly from one year to another? If two households with the same number of members have the same income, are they the same? What if there is one income earner in one household, but two in the other? What if income is from paid work in one household, but results from investments in the other? Should income from manual labour in a dangerous industry be considered the same as that from a white collar job? Consider also when one household rents its accommodation whereas the other has freehold ownership? In this case, the home owning household pays itself an "imputed rent" on its home, which may not be recorded as income. The income measure could be income as declared for tax purposes, income including an estimate of the value of state provided goods and services (health care, education, law and order, street lighting), after tax income, income including estimated accrued capital gains, income including realised untaxed capital gains. More generally, what if there are wealth differences between the households?

If we choose a variable other than income, what should we use? We could consider wealth, or consumption, or total expenditure, or some general measure of wellbeing or standard of living. The choice can have a significant effect on the results.

When looking for equality of circumstances, should differences in age or health be considered? What about tastes, as when some people have expensive interests whereas others have lower cost interests (and this might have an impact on people's decisions about how hard to work and how much to earn).

In other words, we face major problems even at the first stage of deciding when equal circumstances exist. In practice most of these points are overlooked as we have to accept the limitations of the available data and assume no variation within the specified household types.

Vertical equity

Imagine, now, the additional difficulties we face when attempting to specify an "appropriate difference in treatment" when circumstances differ. This is commonly applied to the question of income tax. A progressive income tax structure is one where the tax paid, measured as a proportion of income, rises as income rises. It is often thought that progressive income taxes can be justified on equity grounds. Is this valid? We would have to believe first, for horizontal equity, that equal circumstances apply when the same income is received by two taxable units (individuals in some countries, or couples in others where income splitting for tax is allowed), and second, for vertical equity, that taxable units with higher income are in fact in a better position. That would justify those on higher income paying *more* tax, but it still does not tell us whether they should pay *a higher proportion* of their income in tax, as occurs under a progressive tax.

Older economics literature on taxation attempted to identify equitable tax contributions based on ability to pay, or the "sacrifice" that people make in terms of utility foregone due to the reduction of disposable income due to taxation (Young, 1990). The approach relied on interpersonal comparisons of utility. In it the extent of sacrifice depends on both the amount of tax paid and the marginal utility of income at various income levels. Also, the concept of equal sacrifice is not uniquely defined. To give three possible approaches, we could consider equal absolute sacrifice (everyone gives up a specific number of "utils"), equal proportionate sacrifice (everyone gives up a fixed proportion of their "utils"), or equal marginal sacrifice (the marginal utility of the last dollar paid in tax is the same for all tax payers). Equal marginal sacrifice with identical marginal utility of income schedules involves the dubious outcome of a 100% tax rate on all income from some critical level upwards and 0% tax rate below that level. Whichever approach we choose, we would still have to consider cardinal measures of utility, making interpersonal comparisons. Economists have recognised the difficulties this entails, hence the concepts of Pareto optimality and Pareto improvements to compare options [see No.19].

Unfortunately, even after making all the required assumptions including that of all people getting the same utility from any given level of income, we still do not get definitive results. It turns out that the desirability of alternative tax structures (proportionate, progressive, or regressive) depends on the specific shape of the marginal utility of income schedule. If we reject interpersonal comparisons we cannot even say this. If we add in the possibility of endogenous preferences, then the problems become even more complex.

The benefit principle

There is another perspective that can be taken to consider whether a tax structure is equitable. This is described by the **benefit principle**. It takes into account the effects of expenditure funded by tax revenue. To give a simple illustration, consider a society in which education and health care are provided to all by the government, paid for out of tax revenue. Compare this to another in which these services are only provided to those on low income, with higher income families purchasing these services privately. Would it be equitable for the two societies to have the same income tax scales?

The idea behind the benefit principle is that government intervention in the provision of goods and services can be due to the market failing to adequately express demand. We see this most clearly in the case of pure **public goods**, with their characteristics of **non-excludability** and **non-rivalry** (street lighting is a common example). To correct for this market failure, the government has to act as a vehicle for the expression of demand. It can do this by purchasing the goods or services on behalf of consumers, or it could go a stage further and actually provide them itself, although direct provision of public goods is not strictly necessary.

If the objective is to overcome the failure of the market in expressing demand, the purpose of taxation is to substitute for the market as a means of obtaining payment from the consumers of the goods and services. An equitable tax structure would therefore reflect individual demand as it might have been expressed through functioning markets. Note that this would not result in any redistribution of income between people as they are simply paying for what they receive.

It would be hard to apply the benefit principle accurately as it requires taxes to be tailored to individual preferences. We do not have this information, and it is questionable whether people would reveal the information honestly, due to the **free rider** problem. It does serve to highlight another dimension to the horizontal and vertical equity issue, however, namely the importance of considering not only the relative size of individual contributions, but also the benefits received from the use of the contributions. There are two distinct objectives, one being redistribution and the other being provision. Both of these should be considered when judging whether policies are equitable.

Framing can be important, as observed in some public policy debate. For example, it is sometimes argued that benefit payments or tax concessions should not be made for children from high income households. The argument used is that low income people would be subsidising those on high income and that is unfair. It can be questioned on at least two grounds. First, the reasoning considers a single component of expenditure rather than the overall pattern of revenue and expenditure. Second, it does not make a comparison between high income households with and without children. Vertical equity might suggest that these households are different in composition and so should be treated differently.

There are two ways that we could interpret the above discussion on equity. One is to say that economics cannot help us to determine what is equitable. The other is to say that economics has shown that equity is a complex concept. It may not be possible to find workable definitions of equity, and so those who advocate policies on equity grounds may not have a firm basis for their position.

27. Income distribution measures, the Lorenz curve and the Gini coefficient

A common way to graphically represent income distribution and inequality is by means of a Lorenz Curve as illustrated below. This plots cumulative share of total income on the vertical axis and units of population ordered from lowest to highest income on the horizontal axis. Alternative measures for the vertical axis include disposable income, disposable income plus a measure of benefits in kind (such as education and health care), consumption, or wealth. Units on the horizontal axis could be individuals, income earners, households, or "household equivalents" [see No.26]. For all of these, units would still be ordered from smallest to largest on the horizontal axis according to whatever measure has been chosen. In any event, there are problems with units on the horizontal axis because income, wealth, or consumption may well be shared across units, whether individuals within a household, or across households themselves.

Figure 7 The Lorenz Curve

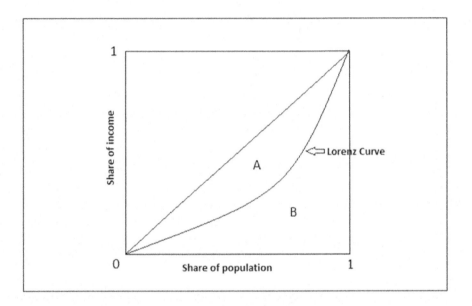

The straight diagonal line in the diagram is the line of perfect equality where, for any value of X from 0 to 1, proportion X of units have proportion X of income. Any inequality will result in a line that drops below this diagonal as indicated. The diagram shows the standard representation of the curve, but in practice we may find some individuals or units experiencing negative income for a given period of time. Consider someone who is self-employed and whose expenses outweigh income, or the owner of a loss-making business. This is very inconvenient and generally ignored. Consequently the line starts at the origin and ends at the top right-hand corner (with all income allocated over all units).

Often data are grouped, with the average income for the group being applied to all in the group. This can avoid the negative income problem if the lowest income group is inclusive enough. However, as you might imagine, this understates the overall inequality by giving straight line segments to the curve.

While a curve lying below the diagonal indicates inequality, we might be concerned to know how unequal the distribution is. This gives additional problems. What is an acceptable level of inequality? In addition, we may wish to compare two distributions to see if one is more unequal than the other.

There is a measure, the Gini Coefficient, that is related to the Lorenz Curve. In the diagram there are two areas marked A and B. Area A will disappear (or equal zero) under perfect equality. Area B will disappear under perfect inequality (where one unit has all the income and all others have nothing). The Gini Coefficient is equal to A/A+B. Grouped data estimate this value on the basis of a piecewise linear approximation of the Lorenz Curve. This gives a number, perhaps 0.3 or 0.4. Is this a high level of inequality? If we compare two distributions and one has a coefficient of 3.3 and the other of 3.5, is this a big difference in inequality? We do have some difficulty in drawing conclusions on either of these points.

The graph gives a two-dimensional representation of the distribution, whereas the Gini Coefficient gives only one number. This means that some information is lost when using the coefficient. If one Lorenz Curve is never above another but, in some places is below the other, then it could be unambiguously stated that it represents a less equal distribution. However, there could be many cases where two Lorenz Curves cross, each being lower at some point. Consider a special case where, for identical Gini Coefficients, one curve is lower for low income households and the other is lower for high income households. Using the coefficients alone, we would say that there is no difference in inequality, however the first has more units who are on relatively low income whereas the other has a few units that are on exceptionally high income. We may see one of these as more of an issue than the other, or, at least, the concerns raised would be different. These problems are not observable when just using Gini Coefficients, so, to interpret the coefficients it may be necessary to draw the Lorenz Curves. If that is the case, we could ask if anything extra is gained by using the coefficients.

There are additional problems to consider. Where units are households, even if we assume that individuals stay all the time in one household and there are no unidentified financial transfers across households, differing household composition requires that some household equivalence adjustment should be used. However, the same equivalence scale cannot be used for adjustments irrespective of the income measure (before tax, after tax, including financial benefits and benefits in kind, etc.).

Sometimes the aim of the research may be to consider the distributional effects of policies, as with a comparison of before- and after-tax incomes. This is problematic because tax paid may not relate solely to income level. Consequently the ordering of units from lowest to highest income may be different on the two measures. Published data are generally grouped and are ordered on one measure only. Consider one curve giving total income and another curve on the same household ordering but just considering benefit income (unemployment, sickness, disability, family, old age, etc.). Low income households are likely to receive a disproportionate share of benefits, in which case the curve would lie above the diagonal line for low income groups. The curve would not be an accurate measure of the effects, however, because two households on the same low income might receive different amounts in benefits.

In summary, there are standard representations and measures of income distribution and inequality that are used. Their use and interpretation can be problematic. As with any data analysis, it is important to carefully consider the nature of the data and the methods of analysis.

28. Industry concentration

Measures of industry concentration indicate the extent to which an industry is dominated by a few players. The units could be enterprises (i.e. businesses, which could have production activity dispersed over many establishments), or establishments, each of which has a single location (such as a factory). High concentration calculated by establishment may indicate economies of scale in production, with production concentrated in a few factories/plants. High concentration on an enterprise basis may give some indication of monopolistic or oligopolistic market structure. However, there are many aspects to consider before conclusions are drawn from the data:

- There is a difference between the classification systems for industry and for international trade. This suggests that industry groupings may not match the groupings required for markets. Production units are classified by industry. The extent of industry concentration may not be a good indicator of market structure.
- Even within an industry, many products may be produced. Even for the "same" product, such as an article of clothing, there could be a large variety of qualities and styles, each aimed at different groups of consumers.
- Industry classifications include increasing levels of disaggregation.
- A single enterprise or establishment may be producing a range of products. It will be classified under its primary activity. The industry classification may be inaccurate if a single classification does not cover all the activities undertaken. A large unit could be a small producer of many products, whereas a small unit could be a major producer of one or two items.
- Products from different industries may be close substitutes for each other.
- Producers in one country may be competing against producers in other countries, and similarly markets in one country may be supplied by producers in other countries. Even producers who do not export may be part of the "traded goods sector" if they compete against imports (or potential imports). It is therefore not enough to consider only domestic production when considering markets.

- The enterprise structure does not necessarily describe the ownership structure. Several enterprises may be owned, or part-owned, by the same individual or organisation.
- The production structure does not necessarily describe the pattern of control over the production and distribution chain. Large supermarkets may have strong bargaining power over their suppliers, for example. While many fast food chains and car manufacturers have their own outlets or agencies, producers of other goods may be reliant on retailers (such as supermarket chains) to make their products available.
- Geographical classification of production data (by country, say) is a form of aggregation which distorts not only due to international trade. Local geographical factors may also be important. Hair dressers in different cities, or even in different parts of a city, do not compete directly with each other. On the other hand, cellphone manufacturers compete on a global market.
- Market competition may be observed in ways that are distinct from the number of suppliers. For example, much competition in the technology area is in terms of upgrades or new products. This has been described a **creative destruction** (Schumpeter, 1976; Swann, 2015). Also according to the concept of **contestable markets** the threat of entry by a potential competitor can affect an incumbent supplier's behaviour, even if that supplier has a monopoly (Baumol *et al.*, 1988).

29. Politics

On reflection it may seem strange that a body of theory describes society as if all activity can be conducted through markets. Political activity is then little more than a footnote when referring to some exogenous government intervening to correct for market failures. This frames the issue in a specific way. To see this, note the following quote from a book by Avinash Dixit:

> "...the traditional dichotomy of markets versus governments, and the question of which system performs better, largely lose their relevance. Markets and governments are both

facts of economic life, and they interact in complex ways. We cannot find feasible improvements by wishing away one of the components."(Dixit, 1996, p. xv)

Institutional economics also highlights the importance of institutional structure, including government institutions, in shaping economic behaviour. Hodgson (2007, p. 326) writes critically of a view of markets which starts with exogenous individuals:

> "...the market itself is an institution, involving complex rules. In reality, markets involve social norms and customs, instituted exchange relations, and information networks that have to be explained... Markets are not an institution-free beginning."

Hare (2012) provides an entertaining read on the importance of institutions in shaping events in the so-called transition economies of the former Soviet Union.

In reality politics and political processes are very important. At the very least, the idea that the economy is a collection of markets independent of government is hard to sustain when you consider how many people are employed in the public sector and how much is spent on goods and services produced by the government sector. Politics is also important in the process of policymaking. While economic theory might suggest particular policy options in response to some perceived problem, actual decisions are the result of political processes. Of course, the news media may also play their part. This means that a purely economic interpretation of an issue may omit important dimensions.

30. Democracy

Just as markets are presented as being effective allocators of resources (frequently with reference to an invisible hand), so are democracies presented as the appropriate form of government. It should be noted that there is no single form of democracy. There are different voting systems (first past the post, proportional representation, single transferable vote, etc.), each with their own implications. Some countries have presidents, some have a one house parliament, others two houses, some have federal systems. The division of powers between institutions and between central, regional and local governments differ. Societies also vary. Some are relatively homogeneous, whereas others have significant ethnic or religious divides (consider the difficulties of a parliamentary democracy in Northern Ireland). Some countries have a long, stable history with established traditions and institutions, whereas others may be newly established, or emerging from a colonial past, or the product of recent civil wars. Religion may be politically important, or its political power may be strictly circumscribed. Moreover, within a country the systems may be changing.

Just as there may be competition in markets, there can also be competition in the political sphere. This may include competition between economic interests, as with trade unions, agricultural or key industrial groups, or the financial sector. This can be observed not only through political platforms, but also through lobbying activity. With an interventionist government in office, a business may gain as much from lobbying activity as through product marketing. Financial institutions may even occasionally receive bailouts when they get into difficulty, especially if they are "too big to fail".

Mainstream economics says little about these areas. There is one finding that you may have come across, however. This is the **Arrow Impossibility Theorem**, a finding from a body of theory that investigated whether it is possible to determine a social preference ordering from individual preferences. You may have come across a more basic but related phenomenon, called the **Paradox of Voting**. The name of the theorem is misleading, and the finding relates to a very special situation.

Consider an individual's ordering of preferences. If option A is preferred to option B and option B is preferred to option C, then we might imagine that the person would also prefer option A to option C. If this is the case, we would say that the preferences are transitive. Otherwise preferences are intransitive (some might say also that they are irrational). It can be shown that, for some patterns of individual preferences, and a particular method of determining social preferences, the resulting social preferences are intransitive.

The method involves binary majority voting (voting over two options at a time where the social preference is awarded to the option with most votes). This conclusion requires both a suitable pattern of individual preferences and the specified voting rules. Rather than an Impossibility theorem, it is more of a "not guaranteed" theorem. We cannot be sure that a voting system will be a satisfactory mechanism for determining society's preferences.

There are many other reasons to be concerned about the results of voting, and this aspect may be a relatively minor importance. For example, often lobbying and negotiating between groups for support can be observed in real world voting processes prior to a vote. This dimension is missed when fixed preferences are assumed. Strength of preference cannot be conveyed through a vote, and people may have one vote every few years although there are many issues and a dynamic policy environment as circumstances change.

The processes in the real world have a major impact on resource allocation and social wellbeing. It could be helpful to give more consideration to politics and its interaction with the economy. At one time political economy was an important area of study. In recent decades a narrower more abstract form of economics has come to dominate.

31. Administration, compliance and law

Policy implementation is not a costless process. Costs incurred by the government in administering a policy are called **administration costs**. Consider the tax system. For every dollar of tax collected the government incurs some costs in the collection process. Staff are employed, computer systems and data bases are set up, resources are allocated to collection, detection of fraud, resolving disputes on tax obligations, and so on. Property taxes are generally considered to have low administration costs per dollar collected, whereas the opposite is the case for capital gains tax. The higher the costs, the less money there is available for other uses.

Costs are also incurred by tax payers in meeting their obligations. Tax returns have to be filed, perhaps accountants and auditors engaged to work through complex issues or to meet legal obligations (as for listed companies). These costs are termed **compliance costs** (Sandford, 1981). It may be possible to reduce administration costs by shifting the burden to taxpayers in the form of compliance costs, so it is not enough to suggest that low administration costs are desirable. One example of this is a value added tax. Registered value added tax payers have to file regular returns and meet the accounting and recording requirements imposed on them by this tax. This reduces costs to government. As Sandford describes, however, there can also be benefits from compliance activity. Companies paying value added tax may find that they have better and more frequent data on the state of their business.

There are other notable economic dimensions to legal obligations. While economic textbooks may refer to laws and regulations (including price controls, workplace safety, product standards, vehicle speed and drink-drive restrictions) as mechanisms for policy, issues of administration and compliance may get little or no attention.

We could look on regulations as binding requirements and assume that everyone is compliant at no cost to them or to the state, but this is unrealistic. One viewpoint is that fines, for example, are prices that are paid on some occasions for certain behaviours. We could even compute an expected fine, given an estimate of the probability of being penalised. From this perspective, if the benefits from the behaviour exceed the fine (or the fine and associated compliance costs), then the behaviour is justified. If some people are law abiding and others take this view, then the latter group have additional options and may be able to out-compete the others. If more people take the latter view, then the administrative costs rise, whereas if everyone is law-abiding then there is little more administration required than education, signage, etc.

The law is important in other ways also. We could view lawyers, the courts, the police and others associated with these activities as providing a service that individuals and taxpayers purchase. On that basis it could be asked what exactly is produced, what are the characteristics of the product, is it produced efficiently in the right quantities, how is the production allocated over individuals, are there externalities, etc. These questions are rarely asked, even in the dedicated field of "law and economics".

Policy

Policy applications

32. Unemployment measurement issues: frictional, structural and cyclical

For economics purposes, we might want to define someone as unemployed if he/she is "in the labour force but not in a job". To be more precise, the person is:

(i) able and (ii) willing to work (iii) at the going wage, but not in a job.
Note the term, "at the going wage". A person's willingness to work may depend on the wage being offered. A crucial issue is whether the going wage is appropriate. Do unemployment numbers change as you change the going wage? That question is not addressed in this approach, although we would expect some relationship to exist. There is a practical reason why this is ignored. To analyse the real world unemployment position we have to use available data. Unemployment numbers reflect the situation at the prevailing wage rates. Note also that measured and actual unemployment numbers may differ.

There are four types of unemployment in the traditional classification. Three of these, frictional, structural and cyclical, will be discussed here. The fourth, seasonal, arises from seasonal fluctuations in labour demand (e.g. fruit picking or tourism) or in labour supply (e.g. school leavers). This will not be covered. Frictional unemployment is occasionally called search unemployment as it is related to the search process undertaken by potential workers and prospective employers. Cyclical unemployment is sometimes called "demand deficient" unemployment because it relates to a low demand for labour.

A very basic representation of unemployment can be given in a supply and demand diagram of "the labour market". It is basic because such a diagram assumes homogeneity of labour. This means that it cannot be used to represent structural unemployment because that is based on there being different types of labour and jobs. It also cannot be used to consider frictional unemployment because it is a static model and does not incorporate adjustment processes (this is a general limitation of such models, so search for any good or service is not considered in these models).

The above paragraph highlights one aspect of the theoretical distinction between macroeconomics and microeconomics. While unemployment is often considered to be a macroeconomic policy issue, as soon as we begin to look at types of unemployment we find ourselves bringing in microeconomic considerations, with disaggregation and analysis of individual markets. The theoretical macro-micro distinction refers to the form of simplification and the types of analogy used. These do not define the nature of the policy issues and related policy solutions. A compartmentalized approach to policy based on theoretical distinctions may lead us to oversimplify and to overlook important dimensions.

There are advantages in the traditional classification of unemployment. Consider a situation where there are unemployed workers and there are job vacancies. The number of unemployed may not equal the number of vacancies, and there are a number of sub-markets reflecting different skills, locations, etc.. For **frictional unemployment** it is possible to match workers and available jobs. The unemployed have desired characteristics for the available vacancies, such as having the right skills and being in the right locations. This would not generally be the case for all unemployed and vacancies. The traditional definition of **structural unemployment** then considers situations where it is not possible to match the unemployed to available vacancies.[11] There are still vacancies, but not for the type of workers available. Hence workers could have the wrong skills (postal

---

[11] Note that this is not the same definition as in Mankiw's *Principles* texts Mankiw, N. G. 2015. *Principles of macroeconomics*. Mason, OH, South-Western Cengage Learning. Available: 6th edition:
http://encore.massey.ac.nz/iii/encore/record/C__Rb2418160?lang=eng.

workers rather than teachers, say) or be in the wrong location. **Cyclical unemployment** then considers the difference between the number of unemployed and the number of vacancies. Even if all vacancies were filled, there may still be some unemployed.

This is summarised in the following table:

Unemployment types

Type of unemployment	Vacancy exists?	Vacancy matches?
Frictional	Yes	Yes
Structural	Yes	No
Cyclical	No	-

The classification is useful because each type suggests distinct problems and associated policy options. Put briefly; for frictional unemployment, improve the search process; for structural unemployment, change the characteristics (e.g. skills, location) of unemployed workers or unfilled jobs; and for cyclical unemployment, create more jobs.

For practical purposes, precise measurement of each type of unemployment can be difficult, complicating the policy maker's task. We can see this if we consider a macroeconomic perspective. Can we use an aggregate labour market supply and demand diagram to consider cyclical unemployment? It might be thought that a market is at equilibrium if the number unemployed equals the number of vacancies (or, in a housing market, the number of houses for sale equals the number of prospective purchasers, for example). This may not in fact be correct, except under special circumstances. Consider the situation where each week, for a particular type of job, there are a hundred new vacancies, a hundred people enter the market looking for work, and a hundred positions are filled. That certainly means that there is a situation where the number of unemployed is constant. Hence it is a form of equilibrium, but numbers of vacancies and jobseekers need not match. If, say, it takes two weeks to fill each vacancy, but only one week for a jobseeker to find a job, then each week there would be one hundred jobseekers, but there would be two hundred unfilled vacancies (one hundred from the previous week, and another hundred new ones that week). In other words, if the search time for a seller to find a buyer does not match the search time for a buyer to find a seller, then a situation of "balance" does not involve the number of buyers and sellers being equal.

Note that for all types of unemployment we are not identifying specific individuals according to unemployment type. For simplicity, let's directly compare numbers of vacancies and unemployed, ignoring the point in the above paragraph. (This might seem a strange thing to do, but it is only strange if the point has been recognized. There are many hidden assumptions in our thinking due to relevant aspects not being considered.) Then if there are four unemployed teachers, one teacher vacancy and two doctor vacancies, one of the unemployed is cyclically unemployed, but we cannot say which one. Of the remaining three unemployed, one is frictionally unemployed, but again we cannot say which one. The best we can do is to identify numbers of each type, and hence the size of the policy outcome required.

Let's now assume that we can accurately identify the number of additional jobs required to eliminate cyclical unemployment. It is not enough to create this number of additional jobs. While it will eliminate cyclical unemployment, it will not necessarily reduce unemployment by that amount. If the jobs are of the wrong type, for example, it may simply be changing the type of unemployed from cyclical to structural.

Can we accurately identify frictional and structural unemployment numbers? This also is problematic. The determining characteristic is whether a match can be made between an unemployed worker and a vacancy. This depends on the classifications used. Consider location. If we group over large geographical areas we will find many unemployed in the same area as the vacancies, whereas smaller areas will result in more of the unemployed being in areas which do not include suitable vacancies. The same applies for skills, as with teachers overall or teachers classified according to primary, intermediate, secondary, maths, languages, years of experience/seniority, etc.. With a highly disaggregated classification, there will be few frictionally unemployed. With a highly aggregated classification, there will be few structurally unemployed. While the classification affects the perceived magnitudes of the various unemployment problems, they do not necessarily accurately indicate matches between unemployed and vacancies. People may be prepared to travel different distances to work and distances can vary according to where homes and jobs are within and between geographical areas (imagine a home and a vacancy on either side of a regional boundary, as compared to being in the same region but at opposite boundaries).

As an additional problem, we should not simply look at the pattern of structural unemployment and attempt to adjust types to get a match over these workers and jobs. First, there can be long lags in retraining or relocating, or in the creation of new jobs. Second, specific jobs may not be filled by unemployed workers. Instead, they may be filled by workers in existing jobs. Under these circumstances the process may be one of employed workers moving to better jobs (as with promotions), thereby creating vacancies lower down the ladder for less skilled or experienced workers. This process is termed **"filtering"** and may apply in other areas besides labour markets. Housing is one area where it has been suggested.

33. Efficiency wage

One example of a market where a price above the equilibrium is described as being justified is that of an "efficiency wage". It is argued that employers are prepared to pay above the market clearing wage because it gives them greater employee loyalty and more choice over potential new employees. It is interesting because it demonstrates the existence of important criteria that are not covered (i.e. are assumed away) in the standard model. In particular, there may be costs associated with labour turnover. These could include hiring costs, layoff costs, firm-specific training for new employees and disruption to production with changes in staff. Consequently employers may wish to retain existing workers. A more loyal workforce may also be more motivated and hence more productive. This latter point suggests that there is not a fixed relationship between inputs and outputs as assumed in the standard production function where output is a function of quantities of capital and labour inputs. The suggestion that choice of employees might be important reflects the heterogeneity of labour, contravening the basic homogeneity assumption in a supply and demand model.

Given that there are several additional dimensions besides a price signal that could be considered, it is surprising that textbooks have focused only on the idea of an efficiency wage. It may be that the market model, with its emphasis on price and the price mechanism, leads us down this path. However, we could consider a much broader picture.

Consider an employer with objectives of staff retention and employee motivation, commitment and productivity. There are many ways in which this could be achieved, especially if we also consider ways that an employer can attempt to meet employees' objectives. Just as an initial list, we could think of: job security; promotion prospects; training opportunities; flexible hours; child care facilities; pension schemes; health insurance cover; pleasant, safe, healthy work environment; company car; staff cafeteria; longer holidays; shorter hours; company social functions; good company public profile/reputation; share options; travel and/or relocation possibilities.

No doubt you could add to this list. It suggests that simplified textbook models may give plausible explanations of and provide some insights into some real world phenomena, but the framing of the issues may also blinker us and limit the possibilities that we might consider.

34. Rent controls

There is a standard textbook representation of the effects of rent controls on the rental housing market. This is based on the premise that a controlled rent is set below the market equilibrium and maintained there in the long term. As it is possible to adapt more in the long run than in the short run, the effects become more significant over time. Supply shrinks and the quality of available accommodation declines. There is excess demand and those in rent-controlled accommodation are reluctant to move. Non-price competition develops and people attempt to circumvent the controls, as in payment of "key money" for example. The textbook conclusion is that such a policy is likely to have many undesirable consequences and is unlikely to achieve its intended purpose.

Much of this is true if policies are applied as described, but this should not be taken to mean that all controls operate in this way. Misapplication of a policy instrument does not necessarily mean that the instrument should never be used. This point is made in a paper which describes "second generation" rent controls (Arnott, 1995). These are more flexible that "first-generation" controls. They allow rent increases due to inflation, various cost factors, etc.

Given the news media and democratic political processes, policies can be introduced in response to a public outcry about some extreme case that hits the headlines. While addressing the perceived injustice, there can be unintended consequences for others coming under the same umbrella policy. Extreme cases with rental accommodation tend to take the form of poor quality accommodation and heavy overcrowding (often of migrants on low income), yielding a high return to the property owner. Alternatively there may be a sudden influx of people into an area putting great short-term pressure on the rental housing market and spikes in rents.

As Arnott describes the policy responses, second generation controls do not aim to permanently suppress rents. Rather, they aim to offer a viable return while limiting extremes of overcharging and poor quality. Short-term peaks can give a windfall gain to property owners while causing problems for tenants or potential tenants (as the supply will not change much in the first instance). Somewhat smaller rent increases in the short term may still signal the need for an increase in supply, thereby producing the desired investment response. In fact, it could give a better signal than rapidly increasing rents that could fall just as fast if supply expanded too fast (note the **cobweb model**, where next period's supply is based on an assumed continuation of this period's price). [See also No.14.] Adaptive rent controls may avoid some of the extreme fluctuations in the market, resulting in improved overall performance.

One lesson to take from this example is that it should not be assumed that a common finding is universally applicable. A policy option should not be dismissed because of misuse in the past. Applied differently, or under different circumstances, the option may be effective and desirable.

Another aspect of some forms of rent control can be seen in the next pointer [No.35].

35. Price ceilings and floors, capitalisation effects

The standard analysis of price ceilings and floors just looks at a market for the good or service using static analysis. Here is one additional aspect to consider. The production of goods and services involves the use of some durable inputs such as land and buildings. They can be used and provide a return for several time periods. Price controls can affect the earnings of these inputs, including expected future earnings.

Consider rental housing and rent controls as an example of a price ceiling, or farm land and agricultural price supports as an example of a price floor. The effect of price controls is to change the income stream of the asset (rental housing or agricultural land), but the value of the asset is based on the income stream that it can generate. This income stream can be capitalised to give a present value, and this in turn determines the current price of the asset as an investment. For example, price supports could be used to provide higher than free market prices for an agricultural product (say meat, wool or dairy products). If expected into the future, this would result in a higher expected future net income for the relevant farm land and consequently inflated land prices.

If the support scheme is then abolished, expected future earnings would fall, with a resulting fall in land prices. This illustrates the way price supports (or subsidies), when expected to continue into the future, can be capitalised to affect values of durable assets such as capital and land. The reverse process applies with price ceilings, as with rent controls on rental accommodation. If they suppress rents, the expected future income stream is reduced and the present value of the expected future net income stream falls. This would translate into a fall in the market price of buildings used for rental accommodation.

It should be noted that all or most of the impact will be felt by the owners of the assets at the time of the policy change (whether an introduction or a removal of the policy), even though the impact on product markets may be spread over many years. Conversely, expectations of a change in policy may affect expectations of future income streams and hence the prevailing values of the assets. This is one reason why asset markets can be sensitive to both policy changes and expectations of policy changes.

36. Physical life and economic life

Capitalisation

Many items are durable (they last and can be used for some time), so they have a **physical life** of more than one time period. We are able to benefit from them over time also, so they may have an **economic life** that lasts some time. The economic life and the physical life may not be the same. The cost of maintaining an old car in a roadworthy condition may be such that we would no longer wish to use it. A record player may still work, but most music is accessed in other ways. We may choose to replace a camera that uses film with a newer digital camera although the former is still functional.

While increasing maintenance costs may justify the replacement of an existing durable asset, quality changes or the introduction of new products can further shorten the economic life of such an asset. This suggests that new developments, while bringing some benefits, may also carry a cost.

Sometimes the distribution of costs and benefits is such that decisions made in a market environment differ from those that might be made when considering overall social benefits. Consider commercial property, such as offices and shops. While location can be important, the age of such properties can also affect their attractiveness to tenants. Investors who build a new complex on a different site may be able to attract tenants away from existing properties, which then suffer a fall in value and perhaps remain vacant for some time or even have to be demolished. The new development may be profitable, but the development decision would not consider the loss in value of the existing buildings. This can be seen if we consider whether a developer would make the same decision when also owning the existing buildings. This is not to say that redevelopment should not occur as some stage. However, it does indicate that self-interested decisions made in competitive environments may overlook some relevant aspects that would be considered in a more collaborative environment.

We can also think of a "physical life" and an "economic life" for human capital. Just as a new office block may make an existing building redundant even though it is structurally sound, so can skills become redundant. Shorthand typists are no longer required now we have computers and even speech-recognition software for converting speech to text.

Consumption

In economics durability is often taken as a distinguishing feature separating consumption activities from investment activities. Hence the benefits of consumption are considered in terms of utility obtained through the consumption activity. They arise at that time only. This is misleading. Consider family occasions, holidays, countries visited, or even memorable films. We may be affected long into the future by the memories, effects on family ties and friendships, and lessons learned. There is not just the immediate experience, but also opportunities for reflection in the future. There can also be positive and negative effects of anticipation of future activities, or the preparation and saving for such activities. The process of lived experiences is far more than instantaneous consumption, despite the way they are represented in utility functions.

37. Returns to education (private and social)

It is often stated that education is a good investment. Economists use the term "human capital", drawing a parallel with investment in physical capital. It is not quite the same, however, so we should be careful when using the analogy. It refers to the productivity of human beings. Generally people cannot be bought and sold (although there was a relatively high literacy rate among Roman slaves because their owners could get a return on their investment). Human capital can be increased in many ways other than formal education, and the result of a given investment in education varies according to the recipient (due to varying ability, motivation, home and social environment, etc.). Depreciation of investments in education is not tax deductible. The value of the investment can vary according to subsequent experience gained.

Education also serves other purposes in society besides being an investment in worker productivity. There is a custodial role (overseeing children), a social cohesion role (social mixing, spreading common perspectives and values), and it can perhaps also be viewed as a consumption activity.

Private costs and benefits from education differ from those for society as a whole. This is in part due to the partial funding of education by the state and the taxation of monetary benefits received by the individual.

Many studies that attempt to measure the benefits of education focus on earnings differentials according to education. We might expect economists to take this approach given that the variables can be quantified. The calculation is sometimes done at a point in time, such as 5 years after graduating if comparing different qualifications, ethnicities, male versus female, etc.. Regression models may also be used. These also estimate average effects and assume constant differences where a dummy variable[12] is used to indicate the qualification gained. There are some problems with these approaches, such as:

- The difference may not be solely due to education (also ability, for example)
- Different earnings profiles over a lifetime make a simple differential inaccurate
- Differentials can change over time due to technology, tastes, labour market conditions (S and D)
- There may be differences in workforce participation and hours
- Non-monetary rewards may affect choice and earnings

---

[12] A dummy variable for a particular qualification would have a value 1 if a person has the qualification and zero otherwise.

More complex approaches might consider differences in earnings profiles over a working lifetime. These can be combined with estimated costs of education and converted into a net income stream over time. A rate of return can then be calculated, giving an estimate of the rate of return to the investment in education. It still faces the limitation that we only have data for the current population. We do not know what earnings differences will be in the future, and the value of a degree to a 60 year old now may be very different from the value in 40 years' time to someone who is now 20.

Quantitative results also tend to give averages. There can be a lot of variation in outcomes over individuals, not least in terms of some students dropping out or failing to qualify. Indications of high returns for a qualification may also result in more people wishing to obtain that qualification. The increase in supply may then lower the return.

From society's perspective, the measurement is further complicated in that pay may not reflect marginal product and there may be **externalities** from education to consider. For example:

- the effect on the next generation, as with parents' education benefiting children;
- faster innovation;
- better management;
- a more informed electorate;
- lower crime (as education alters relative value of legal versus illegal activity, but note "white collar crime").

Forecasting only works when information from the past is relevant for the future. In times of rapid change and limited experience of the new circumstances it is much harder to know what the future will bring. Current information on returns to education is based on many assumptions and may be of limited value for individual decision making.

38. Age distribution issues, generational transfers, dependency ratios, etc.

Theories of the economy based on autonomous ("atomistic") utility maximising individuals must inevitably fail to consider social dimensions of economic activity, including social aspects of specialisation, exchange and transfers. These phenomena are omitted, and hence fall under the *ceteris paribus* umbrella –they are assumed constant, or they are unimportant for the issues under consideration. Class divisions, ethnic or religious identity, family structures, communities are invisible. However, these are central features for many social analyses outside economics. Let's consider just one or two additional dimensions which could be considered in relation to income distribution. They are important, even though they are not topical now.

Not so long ago there was in many countries a form of unwritten "social contract" whereby taxpayers would cover most of the costs of young people's education, including higher education. In exchange these taxpayers would be supported later in their old age through these younger people's tax payments once they are in work. Patterns of rights and responsibilities such as this can serve as a unifying and stabilising force. The "welfare state" system with governments accepting widespread social responsibility only really rose to prominence in the 20th century. In other, perhaps more traditional societies, the extended family unit could be responsible for such arrangements, in which case the strength of family ties is both important and valued.

Similarly, a society might have a convention that people aim to leave assets for their children when they die, or alternatively, there could be a move towards SKI holidays (**S**pending my **K**ids' **I**nheritance holidays), as is more common now. This may also be partly a result of the more fluid nature of families and relationship property legislation, both of which limit or discourage accumulation. It could be debated whether atomistic representations resulted in people overlooking or undervaluing social relationships and obligations, or if other factors led to this individualistic approach which then made the economic theory appear plausible. However, the wide range of alternative options for social organisation should not be overlooked.

Another dimension that is worth noting given current social changes is that of "marriage as a signal" (Rowthorn, 2002). Briefly, if marriage or its equivalent is a binding arrangement that is hard to exit, then willingness to enter into such a relationship signals a high level of commitment. If a potential partner is signalling high commitment, then it can justify a high level of investment in the relationship in return. Conversely, if separation and divorce are easily obtained and if property transfers are rapid, then relationships become far riskier, especially for someone intending to make a large commitment. This might reduce people's willingness to commit, or the level of commitment that relationship formation implies. This also affects people's planning horizons, with less incentive to take a long-term view.

Migration can also impact on social structures, with questions as to who should be assisting whom when relationship ties and obligations extend across national borders. This suggests a growing diversity of social and ethnic groups and complex patterns of obligations. These may not fit neatly into prevailing political structures. Policies may adapt in response to such changes, as can be seen with some entitlements to pensions and benefits when people spend time outside their country of residence. It may also affect a society's commitment to old people if there are large immigrant inflows and emigrant outflows (with migrants generally being younger, and older people being left behind). Under such circumstances the carers for the older generation may not be from a different ethnic group having other social ties.

Dependency ratios relate to the number of young and elderly per person of working age, or per worker (or perhaps full-time equivalent worker). With an aging population, dependency ratios may rise, at least with respect to the elderly. One policy response is to increase labour force participation rates for those or working age, with the main available target group being mothers of young children. This may be easier to achieve in countries with falling birth rates, but the policies may also be a cause of falling birth rates.

One problem that can result when policy issues are seen from limited theoretical perspectives is that there may be "unintended consequences". These consequences are not foreseen because the framing of the issues overlooks them. The points above are intended to show that additional aspects could be included in an analysis.

39. Measuring unpaid work – what does it tell us?

The omission of unpaid work from national accounts has been criticised frequently in recent years. There are good reasons that can be given as to why GDP may be a poor measure of well-being in a country. However, it is unclear what a measure of GDP inclusive of unpaid work (let's call it GDP+) would actually tell us.

GDP+ would not be a measure of total output because it would only include a measure of the labour component of unpaid work - there is no recognition of the capital used in unpaid work (washing machines, ovens, lawn mowers, etc.).

GDP+ would not be a measure of the contribution of labour, paid and unpaid, because the standard GDP component includes not only payments to labour, but also the return to capital in GDP-covered activity.

GDP+ would not be a measure of efficient use of labour because, even if labour markets operate efficiently, the unpaid work sector has more in common with traditional subsistence sectors where disguised unemployment can occur.

GDP+ would not be a measure of output – unpaid work is measured as an input, not in terms of outputs produced.

Nor would GDP+ be a measure of welfare, because the values of other uses of time such as leisure and "personal care" (as found in time-use surveys) are not included, although these are valid alternatives to paid and unpaid work.

In addition, the standard approach to measuring unpaid work is in terms of time spent on various tasks. This is problematic in that people can undertake several tasks simultaneously. If someone spends an hour care-giving a young child while gardening, would as much be achieved as with an hour of care-giving followed by an hour of gardening? What about an hour of care giving while also undertaking a leisure activity such as watching a television programme? Time-use studies recognise the possibility of simultaneous activities. Sometimes they present data on primary activity, with time-use per day totalling 24 hours but secondary and other activities being ignored. Data can also be presented to include simultaneous activities, in which case total measured hours in a day can exceed 24.

An alternative approach is commonly used. This is to value a cooked meal, say, at the amount someone would have to pay for the same meal in a restaurant, or a clean house at the cost of cleaning services. It can yield large figures, which is frequently the objective [see No.40], but they may overstate the value of the work. People's choices not to purchase such things reveal that either the services are not equivalent, or they are not prepared to spend so much in exchange for the saved time. Their or others' travel time related to the activity would also have to be considered. Either they would have to travel to a restaurant, or a cook would have to travel to their home, for example. The cost of services may also include a return for capital equipment and materials, so the market price of the activity reflects more than the cost of the labour.

While aggregate measures such as GDP may have their limitations, the extension of these measures to include other factors may not be as meaningful as is sometimes made out.

40. Cost of illness and impact analyses

There is a trend towards undertaking studies to identify the "cost of illness" for particular conditions. You are likely to see studies on the costs of workplace injury, alcohol consumption, smoking, family violence, or obesity, for example. Studies are also commonly undertaken to estimate the economic impact of major sporting events and on construction of stadiums. These cost of illness analyses and economic impact analyses have strong political and news media appeal. It is easy to get public outrage and political attention by putting out study findings claiming costs of billions of dollars, or to get support for status projects claiming billions of dollars in benefits. They may actually be commissioned for this purpose.

Inflated figures are not uncommon. Some cost of illness studies actually include the cost of policy responses as part of the cost, as with some domestic violence studies which have included costs of police and court services (Snively, 1994).

The studies are of limited value, though. Cost of illness studies may evaluate lives and workdays lost, for example, but they say nothing about options for reducing the amount of illness, the costs of those options, or how effective they might be. If policies can only partially reduce the costs of illness, then the figures do not demonstrate the benefits that could actually be achieved. If there is nothing that can be done, then the costs of the illness are unavoidable. If policy responses are expensive, then they may be undesirable.

Note in particular that we may not want to reduce costs to zero. Workplace costs could be considered part of the costs of production. We do not argue that realised costs of production, such as the costs of labour, should be zero. Instead mainstream theory argues for marginal cost to equal marginal benefit. The same could be said about workplace accident and illness. If the costs are not included in the production decision, then they could be considered as externalities. Economic theory has suggestions as to how these could be addressed [but see No.20].

Alternatively, if labour is voluntarily provided, then arguably (at least according to mainstream theory) the costs to workers of workplace accidents are factored in to their pay and already accounted for. The "according to theory" qualification is important. "Voluntary provision" of labour is really the result of choices made given prevailing options, but a market-focused economics may not question this. For example, there is no reason why perfectly competitive markets would *necessarily* result in all wage rates providing a standard of living at or above the subsistence level. If wage rates are below this level, we might consider the outcome unsatisfactory even though the labour is "voluntarily provided" at that wage, and some form of intervention may be socially desirable.

There are similar issues with impact analyses. For example, a study of the construction of a sports stadium could result in estimates of the number of jobs, value of ticket sales and number of visitors from elsewhere. Experience has shown that these effects may involve transfer of workers from other jobs, diversion of spending from other activities and deterring other visitors from coming. The net effect may be much less than the estimated figures. Results may also be inflated by including multiplier effects following on from the initial spending. Benefits of the spending may not go to the local population as this depends on the sourcing of the workers, patterns of changed spending and ownership of the companies involved in the activity.

It could be argued that political considerations drive the decisions to undertake studies such as these. The aim is to get a high figure to support the case. Once the numbers are publicised, it can be difficult to resist the pressure to act. This does not mean that good decisions are made. At the very least, care must be taken to understand what the results of impact analyses and cost of illness studies really tell us.

Where to from here?

The 40 pointers should have indicated to you a wide range of dimensions for investigation and interpretation of economic theory and applied analysis. There is a lot more to understanding economic aspects of the world than direct application of economic theory and models. Our data and tools for analysis have their own characteristics and limitations. If nothing else, you should now be aware of many questions you can ask to bring a real world focus into your economic analyses.

Theories and models have their place, but they are inadequate on their own. The way we formulate an issue can shape the conclusions that are drawn. Consequently, mechanical application of standard approaches can be dangerous. When large numbers of students learn the same basic material, a momentum builds up which can be difficult to change. This is one of the reasons why international student initiatives have developed that challenge to dominant conventions. If you are interested in these, take a look at the International Student Initiative for Pluralism in Economics, ISIPE, www.isipe.net, or Rethinking Economics, www.rethinkeconomics.org.

For more reading on the general perspective on economics underpinning these pointers, see my book *Rethinking economics: from analogies to the real world* (Birks, 2015). For a wide range of books investigating alternative approaches to economics, see other publications in the WEA e-books series at: www.worldeconomicsassociation.org/books.

References

Arnott, R. 1995. Time for Revisionism on Rent Control? *The Journal of Economic Perspectives,* 9, 99-120. Available: DOI 10.2307/2138358.

Baumol, W. J., Panzar, J. C. & Willi, R. D. 1988. *Contestable markets and the theory of industry structure.* San Diego [Calif.], Harcourt Brace Jovanovich. Available:
http://encore.massey.ac.nz/iii/encore/record/C__Rb1224314.

Birks, S. 2014. Supply and demand models - the impact of framing. *Real-World Economic Review,* , 67-77. Available:
http://www.paecon.net/PAEReview/issue67/Birks67.pdf.

Birks, S. 2015. *Rethinking economics: from analogies to the real world.* Singapore, Springer.

Carr, E. H. 2008 [1961]. *What is history?* Harmondsworth, Penguin.

Coase, R. H. 1991. *The institutional structure of production - Nobel Prize lecture.* Available:
http://nobelprize.org/nobel_prizes/economics/laureates/1991/coase-lecture.html [Accessed 21 October 2013.

Dixit, A. K. 1996. *The making of economic policy: a transaction-cost politics perspective.* Cambridge, Mass, MIT Press.

Eatwell, J. 1987. Import substitution and export-led growth. *In:* Eatwell, J., Milgate, M. & Newman, P. (eds.) *The New Palgrave: a dictionary of economics.* London: Macmillan.

Friedman, M. 1953. The methodology of positive economics. *In:* Friedman, M. (ed.) *Essays in positive economics.* Chicago, Ill.: University of Chicago Press. Available:

References

http://members.shaw.ca/compilerpress1/Anno%20Friedman%20Positive.htm

Friedman, M. & Schwartz, A. J. 1982. *Monetary trends in the United States and the United Kingdom, their relation to income, prices, and interest rates, 1867-1975.* Chicago, University of Chicago Press.

Hare, P. 2012. Vodka and pickled cabbage: Eastern European travels of a professional economist [Kindle edition]. CreateSpace Independent Publishing Platform.

Hodgson, G. M. 1997. Metaphor and pluralism in economics: mechanics and biology. *In:* Salanti, A. & Screpanti, E. (eds.) *Pluralism in Economics: New Perspectives in History and Methodology.* Aldershot: Edward Elgar.

Hodgson, G. M. 2007. The revival of Veblenian institutional economics. *Journal of economic issues,* 41**,** 325.

Karelis, C. 2007. *The persistence of poverty: why the economics of the well-off can't help the poor.* New Haven, Yale University Press.

Keen, S. 2011. *Debunking economics : the naked emperor dethroned?* London; New York, Zed Books Ltd. Available: http://encore.massey.ac.nz/iii/encore/record/C__Rb2447477.

Kuhn, T. S. 1970. *The structure of scientific revolutions.* Chicago, University of Chicago Press.

Lawson, T. 1997. *Economics and reality.* London, Routledge.

Lawson, T. 2003. *Reorienting economics.* London, Routledge.

Linder, M. 1977. The Anti-Samuelson Volume 2 Microeconomics: Basic problems of the capitalist economy. New York: Urizen Books.

Lipsey, R. G. & Lancaster, K. 1956. The General Theory of Second Best. *The Review of Economic Studies,* 24**,** 11-32. Available: http://links.jstor.org/sici?sici=0034-6527%281956%2F1957%2924%3A1%3C11%3ATGTOSB%3E2.0.CO%3B2-2

Lucas Jr, R. E. 1976. Econometric policy evaluation: A critique. *Carnegie-Rochester Conference Series on Public Policy,* 1, 19-46. Available: DOI http://dx.doi.org/10.1016/S0167-2231(76)80003-6.

Mankiw, N. G. 2015. *Principles of macroeconomics.* Mason, OH, South-Western Cengage Learning. Available: 6th edition: http://encore.massey.ac.nz/iii/encore/record/C__Rb2418160?lang=eng.

Maslow, A. H. 1966. *The psychology of science; a reconnaisance.* New York, Harper & Row. Available: http://encore.massey.ac.nz/iii/encore/record/C__Rb1160955.

Morgan, M. S. 2012. *The World in the Model: How Economists Work and Think.* Cambridge, Cambridge University Press. Available: http://encore.massey.ac.nz/iii/encore/record/C__Rb2511175.

Ojimi, V. 1970. Japan's industrialisation strategy. *In:* OECD (ed.) *Japanese Industrial Policy.* Paris: OECD.

Omkarnath, G. 2012. *Economics: A primer for India.* Hyderabad, Orient BlackSwan. Available: http://www.orientblackswan.com/display.asp?isbn=978-81-250-4632-5 http://www.amazon.com/Economics-Primer-India-G-Omkarnath/dp/8125046321.

Porter, M. E. 2004. *Competitive advantage: creating and sustaining superior performance.* New York, Free.

Rostow, W. W. 1971. *Politics and the stages of growth.* Cambridge [Eng.], University Press. Available: http://encore.massey.ac.nz/iii/encore/record/C__Rb1001603.

Rowthorn, R. 2002. Marriage as a signal. *In:* Dnes, A. & Rowthorn, R. (eds.) *The law and economics of marriage and divorce.* New York: Cambridge University Press.

Sandford, C. 1981. Economic aspects of compliance costs. *In:* Peacock, A. & Forte, F. (eds.) *The political economy of taxation.* New York: St Martin's

Press. Available: http://home.fau.edu/kjakee/web/PolEcy/PDFs/Txn-forte-sandford-Ricketts.pdf.

Schumpeter, J. A. 1976. *Capitalism, socialism, and democracy.* London, Allen and Unwin.

Sen, A. K. 1977. Rational Fools: A Critique of the Behavioral Foundations of Economic Theory. *Philosophy and Public Affairs,* 6, 317-344. Available: http://links.jstor.org/sici?sici=0048-3915%28197722%296%3A4%3C317%3ARFACOT%3E2.0.CO%3B2-Z

Smith, A. 2007 [1776]. *An inquiry into the nature and causes of the wealth of nations.* Petersfield, Harriman House. Available: http://encore.massey.ac.nz/iii/encore/record/C__Rb3161462.

Snively, S. L. 1994. *The New Zealand economic cost of family violence.* Wellington, N.Z., Family Violence Unit, Dept. of Social Welfare.

Steinmo, S. 2008. Historical institutionalism. *In:* Porta, D. d. & Keating, M. (eds.) *Approaches and methodologies in the social sciences : a pluralist perspective.* Cambridge, UK ; New York: Cambridge University Press. Available: http://www.svensteinmo.com/articles/Steinmo_2008_historical_institutionalism.pdf.

Swann, G. M. P. 2015. *Common Innovation: How We Create the Wealth of Nations.* Cheltenham, Edward Elgar.

Tinbergen, J. 1952. *On the theory of economic policy.* Amsterdam, North-Holland. Available: http://encore.massey.ac.nz/iii/encore/record/C__Rb1203408.

Vane, H. R. & Thompson, J. L. 1993. *An introduction to macroeconomic policy.* New York, Harvester Wheatsheaf.

Young, H. P. 1990. Progressive Taxation and Equal Sacrifice. *The American Economic Review,* 80, 253-266. Available: DOI 10.2307/2006747.

CPSIA information can be obtained
at www.ICGtesting.com
Printed in the USA
LVOW04s0202160716

496558LV00004B/96/P

9 781848 902176